WHAT DIRECTORS NEED TO KNOW

WHAT DIRECTORS NEED TO KNOW

CAROL
HANSELL

CORPORATE
GOVERNANCE

2003

For our clients.

Design by Bruce Mau Design Inc., Bruce Mau with Barr Gilmore,
Judith McKay and Cathy Jonasson.

Typography by Archetype, Toronto.

Cover photography by Lorne Bridgman.

This publication is designed to provide accurate and authoritative
information. It is sold with the understanding that the publisher is not
engaged in rendering legal, accounting or other professional advice.
If legal advice or other expert assistance is required, the services of a
competent professional should be sought. The analysis contained herein
represents the opinions of the author and should in no way be construed
as being either official or unofficial policy of any governmental body.

The National Library of Canada has catalogued this publication as follows:
Hansell, Carol
    What Directors Need to Know: Corporate Governance 2003 / Carol
Hansell.

Includes index.
ISBN 0-459-28427-4
1. Directors of corporations – Canada. 2. Corporate governance – Canada.
I. Title

HD2745.H35 2003   658.4'22'0971   C2003-902586-1

One Corporate Plaza   Customer Service:
2075 Kennedy Road   Toronto 1-416-609-3800
Toronto, Ontario   Elsewhere in Canada/U.S. 1-800-387-5164
M1T 3V4   Fax 1-416-298-5082
                             World Wide Web: http://www.carswell.com
                             E-mail: orders@carswell.com

Contents

PART I

The Basics of Being a Director

PART II

How the Corporation Works

PART III

How the Board Works

PART IV
Standards of Performance

APPENDIX

2002 / 2003 in Review

Acknowledgements

Corporate governance does not exist in a vacuum. It lives in the context of a corporation's objectives and the actions it takes to advance those objectives. For me, the best education about governance has come from my clients. Over the years, I have had the opportunity to work with some outstanding companies, both large and small. More importantly, I have had the privilege of working with business leaders and corporate counsel who are guided by a strong moral compass. The integrity of the individuals involved in making corporate decisions — much more than the structures and processes discussed in this book — is the foundation of good corporate governance.

This work has benefited greatly from the comments of a number of friends and colleagues who were very generous with their time in reading early drafts. Thank you to David Anderson, Jim Arnett, Brian Bawden, John Bishop, Brian Brown, Bill Dimma, Michael Disney, Robin Fillingham, Paul Fisher, Jim Goodfellow, Gordon Hall, Richard Leblanc, Marcelo Mackinlay, Shawn McReynolds, Rosemary Newman, Keith Robson, Jay Swartz, Larry Tapp and Seymour Trachimovsky. Particular thanks to Jim Gillies, David Jamieson and Jamie Johnson. The final product improved enormously as a result of their comments.

This book was originally written in Saint John, New Brunswick. I am grateful to Susan Menzies and Doug Shippee for the hospitality that made it possible for me to write the first draft. It was largely completed in Hohenlimburg, Germany. Thank you to Karl and

Marieluise Ebbinghaus and to Ulrike Ebbinghaus for their endless generosity and friendship.

I have had tremendous support and patience from Todd Pinsky, Luisa Moncado and Ken Mathies of Carswell from the moment we first discussed this project. Cathy Jonasson, Barr Gilmore and Judith McKay of Bruce Mau Design have brought the book to life with their design and layout (thanks to Roland Semprie for bringing us together). I would like to thank Lorne Bridgman for the beautiful photograph that appears on the cover of the book. Thank you also to my graduate college, Massey College at the University of Toronto, for allowing us access to the Round Room for the photo shoot. I am also grateful for some very insightful advice from Dan Bereskin of Bereskin and Parr and from Ron Blunn of Blunn and Company Inc.

Thank you to my firm, Davies Ward Phillips & Vineberg LLP, for the atmosphere of support and encouragement which makes the conception and completion of a project like this possible. Paul Carder's strategic advice was an enormous help as we were bringing this project to completion. Eric Leduc provided invaluable research support. MaryAnne Kneif's careful proofreading saved me from many fatal errors and Joan Hamilton provided me with very reliable word-processing support every evening. Most of all, thank you to Patti Vanderdonk, my secretary and friend for the past 13 years.

Again, and as always, thank you to my husband, Ron McLaughlin, whose support makes everything I do possible.

Foreword

In the 1950s, when asked about the value of the directors to the company, Irving Olds, Chair of the United States Steel Corporation, responded that they were somewhat "like parsley on fish — decorative but useless." And, interestingly, for most of the period after the end of World War II until the 1990s, his description of the role of directors was exceptionally accurate. For that long period, there was little interest in directors and boards. Retiring chief executive officers, who wrote self-laudatory books about their careers, nearly always referred to the companies that they led as "their company" and seldom if ever referred to the board. Academics writing textbooks about management devoted, at best, one or two pages to the role of the board; there were no courses in business schools on corporate governance until the 1990s and, in fact, hard as it is to believe given the plethora of books on the topic in the past few years, the first general book on corporate governance in Canada was not published until 1992.

And yet, ever since business firms have been organized as corporations, distinct and different from their owners, the need for some group, other than the management, to represent the interests of the owners in the operations of the enterprise has been recognised. In time such groups, who were charged with the responsibility of choosing the chief executive officer, monitoring the activities of the management and generally seeking to protect and hopefully increase the value of the investment of the shareholders, became known as the board of directors.

Needless to say, the delineation of the special duties of boards and an understanding of the optimum relationship between boards and management did not spring up full-blown overnight. Rather they evolved, as did the corporation itself, over time as the result of experience, court decisions and the law. What is striking, however, given the enormous changes in business and industry over the past two centuries, is that the primary roles and responsibilities of directors have not changed much in the past 250 years. Today, the same as at the time corporations were first organized, directors are ultimately responsible for overseeing the affairs of the enterprise. In the process of doing so, it is expected that they will act honestly, be loyal to the organization and will use the care, skill and diligence in fulfilling their obligations that prudent persons would use in managing their own affairs.

Given their long history and great legal importance, why was there such indifference to boards and directors during most of the last half of the twentieth century? The reason is clear. During that period, as corporations grew in size and the number of shareholders multiplied into the thousands, the separation between ownership and management became very wide. Shareholders began to think and act more like investors than owners and left the power of nomination of directors, and even the election of directors, to management. As a result, instead of the shareholders, through the directors, controlling management, the process was reversed. Management, through shareholders' proxies, controlled the election of directors. Since directors were much more beholden to management than to the shareholders for their position, they did, in many cases, become "like parsley on fish—decorative but useless." It is not so astonishing that directors were ignored—they deserved to be. The directors did not responsibly exercise their duties either to the corporation or to its shareholders.

So why have things changed? Business organizations are still large; indeed with the development of the transitional firm they are bigger than ever—some have sales larger than the gross national product of certain countries. Surely the separation of ownership and control is greater than it has been in the past and the power of the directors to act effectively more limited?

There are several reasons why this is not so. First and foremost, doing any type of business anywhere in the world has become dramatically more difficult. With the advent of instantaneous communication, rapid modes of transportation, and most importantly, the decline in barriers to trade, even firms not selling into international markets cannot escape the consequences of freer trade. If a company is less efficient than other companies in the same business anywhere in the world, it soon finds itself faced with strong competition in its own domestic market. There are few tariffs to protect it. As a result, business is a great deal more competitive than at any time in history. To survive successfully, managers need all the help they can get in formulating strategies and managing operations. The most effective place for them to obtain such assistance is from a well-organized, hard-working, involved board of directors. It is a short-sighted, and almost certain to be a short-serving, chief executive officer who does not want a board that is helpful and effective.

Second, as a result of the great increase in the size of pension and mutual funds, there is a much greater concentration of share ownership. Institutional investors, who have no role in managing a specific company, but a very large stake in its success, are insisting that companies be run well. If they are not, they look to the board to improve performance. If a board does not act, institutional investors can change it by voting their huge blocks of stocks against the incumbents. Boards now have to be accountable, in a way that they have not been since the age of the small enterprise in the nineteenth century, to their companies' owners — the shareholders.

Third, there have been, throughout history and including the first part of the twenty-first century, some mammoth corporate failures. Today's shareholders are sophisticated and informed. When a business plummets, they want to know what went wrong and they look to the boards for the answer. If they conclude that the board acted improperly or did not fulfil its duties the shareholders are more and more likely to sue the directors for restitution of their losses. The possibility of litigation does much to focus the mind of board members on their obligations and responsibilities.

The significant point, however, is not that the activities of boards and their *de facto* power vacillate over time. Rather, what is important to remember is that through war and peace, through depression and prosperity, through technological change and institutional reform, through periods when markets are in turmoil and when markets are quiet, when business management is under attack and business leaders are heroes, the fact remains that over a very long time—more than two hundred years—the principles of sound, solid corporate governance have not changed dramatically. Consequently, any burgeoning director and any active director who has a firm grasp of the basic principles of corporate governance as they have evolved through time can be reasonably confident that he or she is well prepared to be not only a competent, but an outstanding director.

Nowhere is there a better place to learn what those principles are, and how they have been modified and developed over the years, than in Carol Hansell's *What Directors Need to Know: Corporate Governance*. Ms. Hansell, the author of *Directors and Officers in Canada: Law and Practice* (Carswell, loose-leaf), the standard legal text on the topic, has brilliantly distilled the essence of the director's duties and responsibilities, both in law and in practice, into this well-written, easy to understand, lively, comprehensive book.

The book lives up to its title. It does, in fact, contain everything that directors need to know about corporate governance. For everyone aspiring to be in the boardroom who wants to know what corporate governance is all about, and for current board members, veterans or rookies, who wish to increase their knowledge about governance, this is the book to read.

James Gillies
Professor Emeritus
Schulich School of Business
York University
Toronto, Ontario
July 2003

Introduction

Directors of Canadian corporations face significant challenges today. Many of these challenges are the same as they have always been. Others are the result of the crisis in investor confidence brought about by corporate failures in the United States, Canada and elsewhere in the last few years.

This book introduces directors of Canadian corporations to basic concepts in corporate governance, with particular emphasis on their own duties and responsibilities. It is intended to provide new directors with an introduction to important principles and to offer more seasoned directors a renewed focus on core issues. While this book is written largely with directors of private sector corporations (both publicly traded and privately held) in mind, most of the concepts are also applicable to directors of public sector and not-for-profit corporations.

Describing a concept in a way that is completely accurate from a legal perspective often comes at the expense of readability. In order to make the concepts in this book more accessible, the legal principles are broadly stated. The book does not deal with technical aspects of the law or the nuances that may be important in particular circumstances. Directors should obtain specific legal advice about their duties and liabilities in connection with each board on which they serve and in the context of particular issues as they arise. A more detailed consideration of the topics discussed in this book can be found in Carol Hansell, *Directors and Officers in Canada: Law and Practice*.

Corporate governance practice and regulations are evolving rapidly as the book goes to print. The text is generally current to June 15, 2003, with an update to reflect certain developments in Canada in June 2003 (see "June 2003 Update").

PART I

The Basics of Being a Director

THE ROLE OF DIRECTORS IN CORPORATE GOVERNANCE

As Enron slid into bankruptcy in the fall of 2001, it had devastating effects on its investors, employees, creditors and suppliers. As monumental as this single corporate collapse was in its own right, it has assumed even greater significance as the first in a series of corporate scandals in the United States involving the misuse of corporate assets and misleading (even fraudulent) financial reporting. Adelphia, Global Crossing, WorldCom and others followed in 2002. What was most disturbing about many of these situations was that directors, senior officers and highly paid advisors — the very people responsible for the decisions that cost others so much — denied accountability and profited with impunity. The resulting crisis in investor confidence prompted the United States government to enact one of the most radical legislative interventions into corporate governance in decades — the *Sarbanes-Oxley Act of 2002*. Other countries, including Canada, have had their share of corporate failures linked to governance weaknesses and are in the process of devising their own regulatory responses.

The focus on corporate governance in what is now referred to as the "post-Enron era" follows a pattern of renewed interest in governance that has occurred after other waves of corporate failure. Similar concerns with governance standards emerged in the early 1990s, following the savings and loans scandals in the United States and the demise of corporate icons such as Royal Trust and Bramalea in Canada. The difference this time has been in the intensity of reaction from the investing public, from government and from securities regulators. This is attributable in part to the number and scale of the corporate failures. However, it also reflects the fact that the impact of these failures has been felt not just by large investors, but by employee shareholders, pensioners and retail investors.

Corporate governance deals with the way in which corporations make decisions. The board of directors sits at the top of the corporation's decision-making hierarchy and so when concerns with governance develop, the way boards make decisions comes under scrutiny. This book deals with what directors need to know about basic corporate governance in order to make an effective contribution to corporate decisions.

WHAT DOES THE BOARD REALLY DO?

Directors are often referred to as "stewards" of the corporation. This is one of many terms used to describe the fact that the legal structure of the corporation separates ownership from management. The shareholders, or "owners", decide who the directors will be, but otherwise have little to do with the way in which the corporation is run.

BEST PRACTICE
_____

TSX Guidelines on the board's stewardship function

The TSX Guidelines refer to the board's overall stewardship function as well as five particularly important aspects of the stewardship function. Guideline 1 states:

1. The board of directors of every corporation should explicitly assume responsibility for the stewardship of the corporation and, as part of the overall stewardship responsibility, should assume responsibility for the following matters:

 (i) adoption of a strategic planning process;

 (ii) the identification of the principal risks of the corporation's business and ensuring the implementation of appropriate systems to manage these risks;

(iii) succession planning, including appointing, training and monitoring senior management;

(iv) a communications policy for the corporation; and

(v) the integrity of the corporation's internal control and management information systems.

What do the directors actually do? The legal aspects of this question are discussed in detail later in this book (see Part II). At a more general level, boards have three basic functions:

1) keeping the right management team in place;

2) approving the direction in which management proposes to take the corporation; and

3) monitoring the way in which management operates the corporation's business.

When the corporation faces particular challenges, the role of the board will of course change (see Part V, When It's Not Business as Usual), but on a day-to-day basis, these are the board's core functions.

The Right Management Team

The board's most important job is to make sure that the corporation has the right chief executive officer. The board is responsible not only for hiring and firing the CEO, but also for approving the CEO's objectives for the year and for incenting, evaluating and rewarding his or her performance.

Many boards appreciate the importance of having a relationship not just with the CEO, but with the other members of the senior management team and often the next levels of management below them. Being acquainted with the individuals responsible for running the company's business gives the board a better sense of the organization. It also allows directors to assess with greater insight both the information and recommendations they receive from management.

Best practice guidelines, including the TSX Guidelines, recommend that the board be involved in succession planning not only for the CEO, but also for the senior management team. This involves an understanding of where the board would look to replace key executives. Would there be internal candidates or would the corporation need to attract someone from outside the organization? The succession planning for the CEO and the rest of the executive team is often part of the mandate of the compensation committee. How involved the board should be in hiring members of senior management other than the CEO can be a difficult question. Many argue that board involvement in senior management hiring decisions infringes on the prerogative of the CEO to put together a team that shares his or her vision. There is, however, increasing acceptance that the audit committee should be actively involved in hiring the chief financial officer and other senior financial executives (whether by approving the selection criteria or the final search candidate or, in some cases, being part of the search committee).

Tone at the top

In the wake of the spate of corporate failures starting with Enron in the summer and fall of 2001 and continuing throughout 2002, "tone at the top" has become an issue of considerable focus. "Tone at the top" means that the board and senior management are responsible for setting the ethical tone for the corporation and for then managing the corporation and its business in a manner that is consistent with that tone. One of the ways in which the board can promote the appropriate "tone at the top" is through the selection and evaluation of the CEO. Another is to satisfy itself that appropriate codes of conduct and compliance programs are in place and are being enforced and that remedial action is being taken as necessary.

Approval of the Corporation's Direction

With the right CEO and management team in place, the board reviews the direction in which it proposes to take the corporation and works through with management any changes it considers necessary. To do this, the board must understand the risks facing the corporation and the opportunities available to it. It then reviews and approves strategic and business plans, capital expenditure budgets and other plans, budgets and forecasts prepared by management. These documents establish the parameters within which management proposes to operate the business in light of the risks and opportunities facing the corporation. If management proposes to take any other significant action which has not been approved as part of this process (or has been approved in principle only), it returns to the board to obtain its approval.

Role of the board of directors in corporate strategy

The role of the board in corporate strategy has received increased attention in recent years. While it is generally the CEO that develops and implements the corporation's strategy, it is important that the CEO have the board's support for that strategy. The board will often be involved in advising the CEO in development of the corporate strategy. Many boards dedicate several days to strategic planning sessions for this purpose. It is then important that the board monitor the implementation of the strategy throughout the year. Many boards do this by including as an agenda item for each board meeting a review of the corporation's implementation of its strategy.

Best practices have long recommended a significant role for the board in corporate strategy — both approving the strategy developed by the chief executive officer and then by monitoring the implementation of that strategy. In 1994, for example, the Dey Report stated:

> The CEO, with the active involvement of the board, is responsible for leading the company into the future and therefore must ensure that there are long term goals and a strategic planning process in place. The leadership for this process must come from management. The board should bring an objectivity and a breadth of judgement to the strategic planning process because the board is not involved in the day-to-day management of the business.

The board must ultimately approve the strategy as it evolves.

The TSX Guidelines (which were drawn from the Dey Report) include the adoption of a strategic planning process as one of the five specific responsibilities which a board of directors should assume as part of its stewardship function.

The NACD released the Report of its Blue Ribbon Commission on The Role of the Board in Corporate Strategy in 2000. One of its key recommendations was:

Boards should be constructively engaged with management to ensure the appropriate development, execution and modification of the company's strategy.

In this report, the NACD cautions directors to be sensitive to crossing the line between effective oversight and micro-management. "An overly involved board can have the unintended consequences of alienating management, undermining management's authority and weakening management responsibility for results." There is also the real possibility that heavily involved directors — if they become too committed to a single strategy — will lose the objectivity that is so important for the oversight function.

Monitoring Management

Once the corporation's course has been set for the year, the board monitors the way in which management operates the corporation's business. The monitoring function occupies the majority of the time that most directors devote to the corporation. It includes reviewing reports on operating results, monitoring internal controls and overseeing the corporation's compliance with legal requirements. It also includes a variety of functions specifically assigned to the board by statute — such as reviewing and approving the corporation's financial statements before they are delivered to the shareholders.

The board's monitoring function includes oversight of the risk management process. There are five steps a board should take in its oversight of most risks:

- Identify the risk — usually it is management, but it may be outside advisors, that identifies and defines risk for the board.

- Evaluate the risk — management, often with input from outside advisors, will evaluate the risk (including quantifying the exposure) in order to determine what type of risk management strategy is appropriate.
- Review the risk management strategy — the board needs to be satisfied with the way in which management proposes to manage each of the principal risks facing the corporation.
- Monitor the risk management process — the board should receive reports from management on the implementation of the risk management strategy. These reports should describe not only major occurrences, but less significant occurrences that suggest a trend.
- Take remedial action — if the board becomes aware of any material breach of the controls put in place or any pattern of immaterial breaches, it should discuss with management whether any remedial action is required in response to these breaches and monitor the implementation and effectiveness of this action.

The board should re-evaluate the risk and the related risk management strategy on a regular basis. This is often done with input from the internal auditor and from outside advisors.

LEADING DECISION

Caremark

The 1996 decision of the Delaware Court in Caremark was an important case in establishing what directors must do to discharge their oversight function.

Caremark International Inc. was subject to certain federal and state laws applicable to health care providers. It was charged with multiple felonies under those statutes. It ultimately pleaded guilty to a felony charge of mail fraud and agreed to pay $250 million in civil and criminal fines and to make reimbursements to various private and public parties. In a derivative action commenced by certain shareholders, the directors were accused of having allowed a situation to develop and continue which exposed the corporation to enormous legal liability, thereby breaching their duty to be active monitors of corporate performance. The derivative action was settled and application was made to the Court for an order that the settlement was fair and reasonable.

The Court stated that there were two bases on which the directors could be held liable for breach of their duty to exercise appropriate attention. First, liability could result from a decision that was ill advised or negligent (but only on the basis that the process used to reach the decision was negligent, not on the basis of the decision itself). Second, the directors could be held liable for their inaction, that is, for a failure to monitor. The Court acknowledged that a board of directors is not typically involved in all corporate decisions, but that it has a duty to ensure that a corporate information gathering and reporting system exists which represents a good faith attempt to provide senior management and the board of directors with information respecting material acts, events and conditions within the corporation, including compliance with applicable statutes and regulations. It held that "generally where a claim of directorial liability for corporate loss is predicated upon ignorance of liability creating activities within the corporation...only a sustained or systematic failure of the board to exercise oversight — such as an utter failure to attempt to assure a reasonable information and reporting system exists — will establish the lack of good faith that is a necessary condition to liability."

The Court reviewed the actions taken by both management and the board of Caremark to prevent the alleged violations from occurring in the first instance and then their response to the investigation by Caremark. Among other things, it found that the systems in place at Caremark that informed the directors about Caremark's activities represented a good faith attempt on the part of the directors to be informed of relevant facts. The directors could not be faulted if they did not know about the specifics of the activities that led to the charges against Caremark.

In re Caremark Intern. Inc. Derivative Litigation, 698 A.2d 959 (Del. Ch., 1996)

THE ROLE AND RESPONSIBILITIES OF MANAGEMENT

This book deals with corporate governance from the perspective of directors. However, many of the same issues discussed here will apply to members of the corporation's management. It is particularly important for senior members of management to understand that they are subject to the same fiduciary duty and duty of care as are directors of the corporation (see Part IV) and must discharge their responsibilities in accordance with these duties.

There are several core distinctions between the role and responsibilities of directors and those of the corporation's officers (i.e., its management team). First, officers (or "management") are responsible for running the company on a day-to-day basis, while the directors monitor their activities. Second, there are certain liabilities to which directors, but not officers, are subject — such as payments to shareholders when the corporation is insolvent (see Part VI) and liability for employee wages. Third, there are certain liabilities to which directors and officers may both be subject, but for which officers are more likely to be held accountable because they are in a better position to control the actions of the corporation in connection with that matter (see discussion of *Bata* case).

THE THREE ELEMENTS OF BOARD DECISION MAKING

There are three elements in any decision the board makes: the information it has available to it, the process it uses to consider that information and the business judgment it applies to that information in the context of that process. Each of these elements is discussed below.

Information

Ordinarily, the board looks to management to provide it with the information it needs in an appropriate form and in a timely manner. It is, however, ultimately the responsibility of the board to be satisfied that it has the information necessary to exercise its business judgment effectively.

Clearly, management has much more information than it provides to the directors. It must determine which information to send to the board and how that information should be presented. How management makes that determination is critical. Some decisions are straightforward. For example, management would not typically send on to the directors information which it found irrelevant or immaterial in its evaluation of a particular matter. Nor does management typically provide the directors with raw data. Instead, it distills and analyzes the information it considers relevant and presents that information to the board in a form that will allow the board to understand the key considerations.

Directors should consider whether the information they receive from management is sufficient to discharge their responsibilities effectively. How much information is enough? Clearly, the directors do not need to see every bit of information that management has available to it. The difference between management's information needs and those of the board reflects the difference between running the business and overseeing the way in which the business is run. Directors should put themselves in a position to understand what information management is relying on and why it led to the recommendation being made. Directors must be satisfied that they receive information in a format that allows them to absorb the key issues and reach informed judgments. They must insist on having sufficient time to review and consider the information they receive. If a board is not customarily receiving from management the timely, accurate and digestible information it requires to discharge its oversight function, it must take action to correct any deficiencies.

When directors do not feel satisfied that they are able to reach an informed judgment with respect to any particular matter, they must seek out whatever additional information they need to supplement or validate the information received from management. Accounting, financial and legal advisors are an important source of information, analysis and perspective, whether they are the corporation's advisors or advisors the board retains specifically for the purposes of advising on a particular issue. Advisors must be experienced and qualified with respect to the issues being considered by the board. In some cases, it may be advisable for directors to obtain advice directly from outside advisors rather than having it filtered through management.

Directors are entitled to rely on the information they receive from management. They may not, however, accept management's analysis and recommendations without question. Directors should understand management's assumptions and analysis and request additional information to the extent necessary. They are not entitled to turn a blind eye if they have reason to believe that management is not being forthright with them. If the directors sense that management is withholding information or misleading them or has some agenda that would influence the analysis it provides to the board, they must continue to probe and investigate until they are satisfied.

Effective directors do not focus exclusively on the company and the results of its operations but instead take positive steps to inform themselves about the industry and broader environment within which the company operates. They develop their knowledge base by reading industry publications and analysts' reports, and by attending trade shows, as well as through their personal contacts. Of course, the board may be in no better position than management to recognize the significance of changes in markets, competitive forces and technology, for the corporation and its prospects. However, directors should not be dependent on management as their only source of information, otherwise they will only be able to interpret external developments exclusively from the perspective of management.

LEADING DECISION

Judicial inquiry into the collapse of the CCB and Northland banks

Many of the highly publicized cases of corporate failure have been characterized by incomplete or inaccurate information being provided to the corporation's unrelated directors. The demise of Standard Trust is one case in point. Another is the collapse of the Canadian Commercial Bank and Northland Bank. The lesson drawn from these situations is that it is insufficient for directors to be passive recipients of whatever information management decides to provide. Directors must satisfy themselves that they are getting the information they need. In his evaluation of the demise of the CCB, Mr. Justice Estey pointed to the lack of information being provided to the board and was critical of the directors for not demanding more:

If there is one key to the troubles encountered by the Board in directing the affairs of the bank, it was their complete failure to insist upon simple and straightforward regular and timely information from management. The institutions and processes were in place in the government [sic] of the bank but they did not function because management did not deliver and the Board did not demand a flow of the basic information necessary to the control of the affairs of the bank and to keep management within the policies as laid out by the Board.

Inquiry into the Collapse of the CCB and Northland Bank, *Report of the Inquiry into the Collapse of the CCB and Northland Bank* by The Honourable Willard Z. Estey (Ottawa: Supply and Services Canada, 1986).

Process

The two fundamental components of board process are independence and diligence.

Board independence is one of the leading themes in corporate governance. The objective is to have directors who are independent minded in the discharge of their responsibilities. Usually the issue is independence from management.

The board's role is to oversee management and if management dominates the board, it is unlikely that board oversight will add anything. A variety of legal requirements and best practice standards operate to ensure that public company boards have a certain number of directors who are independent of management. It is then up to the individual directors to be sure that they are acting in an "independent-minded" fashion.

Independence concerns can go beyond independence from management. When the corporation has a controlling shareholder there may be situations in which board decisions should be made (or at least recommendations formulated) without the participation of the controlling shareholder (or any director with a close relationship with the controlling shareholder). This will be the case, for example, where the corporation is considering entering into a material transaction with the controlling shareholder. There is no reason that the controlling shareholder and the corporation can't do business together, but directors who have no relationship with the controlling shareholder should make the call about whether a transaction involving the controlling shareholder is in the corporation's best interests.

The second component of an appropriate process is the diligence exercised by the directors. What diligence means will depend on the context. As discussed above, directors should be confident that they have received adequate information from appropriate sources (discussed above). They should also be confident that they have taken the time necessary to consider the information before them.

Independence is discussed in more detail in Part III, diligence is discussed in more detail in Part IV.

Business Judgment

Business judgment is the final element in a board's decision-making process. It is a product of the background, experience, insight and instincts of the directors involved in decision making. Corporate governance rules and guidelines cannot create good business judgment, but they can put the directors in a position to apply their business judgment effectively.

The courts have developed a "business judgment rule", which is discussed in Part IV. Essentially, it means that the courts will not second guess the decision made by diligent directors who followed an independent process.

FINDING THE RIGHT DIRECTORS

Each director will bring different skills to the work of the board. No one director will have all of the skills and qualities necessary to discharge the work of the board thoroughly and effectively.

Each time there is an opportunity to recruit a new director to the board, those responsible for identifying potential candidates will need to evaluate the needs of the corporation. The following factors should be taken into account:

* The existing composition of the board — are there any skill sets that are currently lacking?

- The corporation's strategic direction — does the company have plans that would benefit from board input that it does not currently have?
- Board succession planning — are there directors who plan to step down in the near future whose skill sets will need to be replaced?

One of the first considerations in identifying a potential candidate to fill a board position is the business experience that would be helpful to the corporation. For example, the corporation may need specific experience in the industry or sector in which it operates (e.g., telecommunications, packaged goods, natural resources) or in a particular geographic market which it plans to enter for the first time (e.g., the United States or the Far East). If the company is in high growth mode or about to embark on an aggressive acquisition program it may wish to add a director who has experience managing or serving on the board of a corporation going through a similar phase, to its board.

Particular types of management experience may also be desirable. The board may need directors who have had responsibility for financial reporting or who have demonstrated ability in strategic planning. Chief executive officers of other corporations are among the most sought after directors because of the operational experience and strategic vision they are likely to bring to the board. However, many CEOs are reluctant to take on too many outside commitments and many corporations, in fact, restrict the number of outside boards on which the CEO may sit. Executives other than CEOs may also be approached, although many of them will be subject to the same restrictions.

The type of board experience a candidate has may also be an important consideration. Experienced directors will bring with them an understanding of many of the issues dealt with in this book — the way in which a corporation operates, the role of the board and the nature of their duties to the corporation. Directors who have served on public company boards will be sensitive to public disclosure and investor relations issues. The corporation may need someone on the board who understands how to establish objectives for a CEO, how to assess the performance of the management team or how to support management in the development of policy and strategy (rather than focusing on tactics and details which should be left with management in most cases). Finally, if a candidate has board experience, inquiries can be made about whether he or she has contributed effectively as a member of other boards.

Personal attributes are also important. The board should make inquiries about and be comfortable with a candidate's reputation, including his or her ethical standards. It should be clear that the individual has no relationships that would be adverse in interest to the corporation's interests and that he or she has a genuine interest in the company and its business. The board should be confident that the individual will act in an independent-minded fashion and has the temperament that will allow him or her to act effectively as a member of the particular board.

Whether a candidate is willing and able to commit the time to be an effective member of the board is another consideration. Can the director attend meetings of the board as well as any committees on which he or she serves? Is the candidate prepared to sit on the board committees? Does the candidate understand the compensation arrangements for directors?

Finally, boards will need to take into account whether they will be able to satisfy the legal and regulatory requirements with respect to board membership. Public companies are generally required to have a certain number of "independent" or "unrelated" directors. These concepts are discussed in Part III, but generally mean directors who have no relationship with the corporation or its management (other than their positions as directors). In some cases these terms may also mean independence from a major shareholder or significant stakeholder. The board will also need to consider the composition of its committees and whether the candidate will have the independence and qualifications to sit on committees as needed.

Whatever the qualities and experience of the individual directors, the point is often made that colossal corporate scandals such as Enron have unfolded under the supervision of an all-star board, with qualifications far beyond what any regulator would ever impose. As is the case with any other single aspect of corporate governance, the experience and personal attributes of the individuals comprising the board, are not a panacea. They can, however, make a tremendous contribution to effective governance.

Financial literacy

The phrase "financial literacy" was coined by the NACD's Blue Ribbon Commission on Director Effectiveness and was subsequently adopted by the Blue Ribbon Commission chaired by Ira Millstein. The NYSE and Nasdaq now require that all members of audit committees be "financially literate" or must become "financially literate" within a reasonable period of time after his or her appointment to the audit committee.

The New York Stock Exchange does not set out what "financially literate" or "accounting or related financial management expertise" means, deferring to the board of directors of each issuer to interpret such qualification in its business judgment. The AMEX/Nasdaq stipulate that in order to be considered "financially literate", audit committee members must be able to read and understand fundamental financial statements, including a company's balance sheet, income statement and cash flow statement (or become able to do so within a reasonable period of time after his or her appointment to the audit committee).

In Canada, there is not yet a requirement for audit committee members to be financially literate, although the proposed amendments to the TSX Guidelines would expand the guidelines relating to audit committees to provide that all of the members of the audit committee be financially literate. The related practice note states:

> A suggested definition of "financial literacy" is the ability to read and understand a balance sheet, an income statement, a cash flow statement and the notes attached thereto.

See "June 2003 Update" for CSA developments

Financial experts

Both the NYSE and Nasdaq currently require that at least one member of an audit committee be a "financial expert" (although they have different approaches for determining who qualifies as a "financial expert"). These definitions are likely to change in light of the SEC definition of "financial expert", defined below.

The appropriate definition of "financial expert" became the subject of considerable debate after the enactment of Sarbanes-Oxley, which requires companies to disclose whether they have a financial expert on their audit committee and, if not, why not. The definition of "financial expert" first advanced by the SEC set the bar so high that many observed that neither Warren Buffet nor Alan Greenspan would qualify as a "financial expert". In response to these concerns, the SEC revised its definition of "financial expert" (now called the "audit committee financial expert") considerably in its final rule to mean a person with the following attributes:

- an understanding of financial statements and generally accepted accounting principles;
- an ability to assess the general application of such principles in connection with the accounting for estimates, accruals and reserves;
- experience preparing, auditing, analyzing or evaluating financial statements that present a breadth and level of complexity of accounting issues that are generally comparable to the breadth and complexity of issues that can reasonably be expected to be raised by the registrant's financial statements, or experience actively supervising one or more persons engaged in such activities;
- an understanding of internal controls and procedures for financial reporting; and
- an understanding of audit committee functions.

The rule goes on to provide that a person can acquire such attributes through any one or more of the following means:

- education and experience as a principal financial officer, principal accounting officer, controller, public accountant or auditor, or experience in one or more positions that involve the performance of similar functions;

- experience actively supervising a principal financial officer, principal accounting officer, controller, public accountant, auditor or person performing similar functions, or experience overseeing or assessing the performance of companies or public accountants with respect to the preparation, auditing or evaluation of financial statements; or
- other relevant experience.

There is currently no requirement in Canada for any member of the audit committee to be a financial expert, although the proposed amendments to the TSX Guidelines would expand the guidelines relating to audit committees to provide that at least one member of the audit committee should have "accounting or related financial experience." The related practice note states:

> A suggested definition of "accounting or related financial experience" is the ability to analyze and interpret a full set of financial statements, including the notes attached thereto, in accordance with Canadian generally accepted accounting principles.

See "June 2003 Update" for CSA developments.

NACD *on director characteristics and competencies*

The Report of the NACD Blue Ribbon Commission on Director Professionalism, (2001 Edition) recommends that individual directors should possess all of the following personal characteristics:
- integrity and accountability
- informed judgment
- financial literacy
- mature confidence
- high performance standards.

It also recommends that the board as a whole should possess all of the following core competencies, with each candidate contributing knowledge and experience in at least one domain:
- accounting and finance

- business judgment
- management
- crisis response
- industry knowledge
- international markets
- leadership
- strategy/vision.

STAYING ON TOP OF THE ISSUES

Directors are typically recruited to the board for the experience and expertise that they have acquired over the course of their careers. However, there remains a great deal of work to do in order to stay current with evolving expectations of directors and with the changing needs of the corporation.

Director education has been recommended as a matter of best practice in Canada for almost a decade. The foundation of director education is a well thought out orientation program for new recruits to the board. The orientation program should acquaint a new director with the corporation and its business, with key executives and with external advisors who play a regular role with the corporation. Many corporations provide this type of orientation through a very formal program, while others hold *ad hoc* meetings and discussions.

The other component of director education is ongoing education. Some directors are resistant to ongoing education, believing that they are at a point in their careers where this should no longer be necessary. However, the complexity of most businesses and the pressure on boards to be accountable is driving a new demand for director education.

There are a number of organizations which offer director education — universities, conference providers, professional organizations, law firms and accounting firms. The Institute of Corporate Directors* is launching a number of important initiatives that will broaden the range of options for directors seeking to stay current with governance developments. In-house programs designed for a particular

*The author is a director and Vice-Chair of the Institute of Corporate Directors.

board can make the education more focused on the specific issues facing the corporation and on the needs of a particular board. In-house programs, of course, depend on the resources the corporation has available to it to develop and present these programs either entirely on their own or with input from outside advisors and consultants. It may be more practical in many cases for directors to attend programs sponsored by outside organizations.

CURRENT ISSUE

Director education

Director education is the subject of increased focus by stock exchanges. The TSX Guidelines have long recommended orientation and education programs for new directors. Guideline 6 states:

6. *Every corporation, as an integral element of the process for appointing new directors, should provide an orientation and education program for new recruits to the board.*

The amendments being proposed by the TSX in its guidelines would go beyond education for new directors, recommending that "every corporation should provide continuing education for all directors."
In its 2002 report, the New York Stock Exchange Corporate Accountability and Listing Standards Committees recommended that the NYSE take certain initiatives relating to director education. In the second quarter of 2003, the NYSE introduced the Directors' Institute on Corporate Governance, which it describes as a continuing-education forum for current newly elected directors.

WHO EVALUATES THE BOARD?

How do directors know when they are getting it right? Many take the success of the corporation to be the best indication. While this may be a positive sign, that success may have less to do with the board and more to do with the corporation's franchise, management's skill or general market conditions. In a case of a company that is not doing well, it may also be true that an effective board has successfully held it back from the brink of insolvency and deserves credit for the corporation continuing to at least operate as a going concern.

Boards are being encouraged to evaluate their own performance and the performance of individual directors. Although governance reports have advocated board assessment for some time, relatively few boards have implemented an evaluation process in any meaningful way. Regulatory focus on board evaluation in the United States may reverse this trend. The proposed amendments to the NYSE corporate governance listing requirements will require the audit, compensation and governance committees to conduct an annual performance evaluation.

BEST PRACTICE

Director assessment

In the proposed amendments to its corporate governance listing requirements, the NYSE is placing increased emphasis on assessment, both at the committee and the full board level. It will also require listed companies to adopt and disclose their corporate governance guidelines, which must address the annual performance evaluation of the board. The requirements state:

> *The board should conduct a self-evaluation at least annually to determine whether it and its committees are functioning effectively.*

In addition, these proposed amendments will require each of the nominating/governance committee, the compensation committee and the audit committee to address in their respective charters an annual performance evaluation of the committee.

Two of the TSX Guidelines deal with director assessment. Guideline 4 recommends that the committee responsible for appointing new directors also be charged with the responsibility for assessing directors on an ongoing basis. Guideline 5 recommends that a process be put in place for evaluating the performance of the board, its committees and the contribution of its individual directors. Guidelines 4 and 5 state:

4. *The board of directors of every corporation should appoint a committee of directors composed exclusively of outside, i.e., non-management, directors, a majority of whom are unrelated directors, with the responsibility for proposing to the full board new nominees to the board and for assessing directors on an ongoing basis.*
5. *Every board of directors should implement a process to be carried out by the nominating committee or other appropriate committee for assessing the effectiveness of the board as a whole, the committees of the board and the contribution of individual directors.*

Director assessment can focus on the effectiveness of the full board (or a committee) or on the effectiveness of the individual directors. Full board review will often take the form of a questionnaire or one-on-one discussion in which directors are asked if they believe they receive appropriate information in a usable form, whether there is enough time at meetings for discussion, whether management presentations are useful, etc. The full board assessment may be conducted by the corporate governance committee, with support from the corporate secretary. It may also be administered by an outside provider, such as a human resources consultant, under the supervision of the governance committee. The results of the assessment are typically provided to the chair of the corporate governance committee or the board chair, who uses those results to effect improvement in the way in which the board functions.

Individual director assessment is generally done in one of three ways: self-assessment, peer assessment, or assessment by an outside consultant. Like the full board assessment, the process can be carried out by the corporate governance committee or other appropriate committee, or can be administered by an outside consultant under the supervision of the governance committee. The results of the assessment will typically be discussed with the director by the chair of the governance committee (or the board chair) or by a consultant with a view to determining whether the corporation should provide any assistance to the director in operating more effectively.

Self-assessment is generally the least threatening approach to director assessment. Directors rate their own performance according to criteria which have been identified by the corporate governance committee or an outside consultant. Peer assessment involves each director assessing the performance of each of the other directors. Assessment by an outside consultant involves a third party monitoring the performance of individual directors and then providing a view of their effectiveness as board members.

WHAT TO CONSIDER BEFORE JOINING A BOARD

Why Do It?

In today's climate, the down side of being a director gets a great deal of attention. Nevertheless, there continue to be many talented business people who are prepared to serve on boards.

What attracts people to board service? There is a certain status associated with being a corporate director; being invited onto a board is an important milestone in most careers and the appointment to a major public company board represents a significant career achievement. Developing an understanding of a corporation and the environment in which it operates can be both interesting and challenging work. Contributing to the development and execution of a successful corporate strategy and providing support and advice to a highly skilled management team is professionally satisfying. In addition, opportunities to network with board colleagues and senior management can be important from both a business and personal perspective. Finally, the remuneration, in some cases, can be attractive, particularly where directors are granted stock options.

The negative aspects of board service must also be acknowledged. Directors who are doing their jobs effectively will find that it is very time consuming, particularly when they do not yet know the company well. Many boards do not pay much — particularly in light of the experience and seasoned judgment most directors contribute. The decisions of a board may be open to scrutiny by legislators, regulators, investors, media and the public generally.

Directors may be held personally liable for the corporation's actions in some cases. Even if they have done nothing wrong, they can still be sued. Mounting a defence — even a defence that is ultimately successful — is expensive, time consuming and emotionally draining. If the corporation is not required to reimburse the directors for their defence costs — or if the corporation simply does not have the money to pay — the directors must pay for the legal expenses and for any fines or damages assessed against them. This is why directors should have directors' and officers' insurance — and many do. However, there can be situations that the insurance does not cover and again, this can leave the directors paying the bill directly for any legal or other costs they may incur.

Ask the Right Questions

To make the experience of acting as a director as satisfying as possible — and to avoid venturing into dangerous territory in terms of personal liability — prospective directors should consider the following questions before they accept a position on a board:

What do you know about the corporation?
- What type of business is the corporation in?
- Is the corporation and its business of interest to you?
- What potential liabilities do directors face that are peculiar to this company or the industry in which it operates?
- What is the financial condition of the corporation?
- Do you know what the corporation's values are and do they fit with your own?
- What do people who are unconnected with the corporation tell you about their impressions of the corporation and its reputation?
- What does the corporation want you to contribute and are you equipped and prepared to make that contribution?

Are the right relationships in place to allow you to perform effectively?
- Who are the other directors — particularly the other outside directors?
- What is the relationship of the board to any major shareholder?

- What type of relationship does the board have with management, in particular the CEO?
- What type of relationship does the board (or audit committee) have with the external auditor and internal auditor?
- Do you have any other relationships or interests that may conflict with your duty to the corporation?

Do you have the time for this commitment?
- How many board meetings will there be each year?
- How many committees will you be expected to sit on (or chair) and how often do they meet?
- Are the board and committee meetings in town, or will you be required to travel?
- How much time will you need to devote to preparing for meetings and to being well-informed about the corporation and the industry in which it operates?
- How many other boards are you on?
- Do you otherwise have the time to devote to this board?

Consult the Right People

A prospective director should consider meeting with the following people to elicit their view about the corporation, the challenges it faces, the dynamic in the boardroom and the relationship between the board and management:
- chair or lead directors
- chief executive officer
- chief operating officer
- chief financial officer
- other officers as appropriate
- chair of the audit committee
- other directors (and former directors)
- external auditor and internal auditor
- inside counsel
- outside counsel.

Review the Right Documents

A prospective director should also consider reviewing the following:

- financial statements
- press coverage (including trade publications) about the corporation and its competitors
- analysts' reports about the corporation and its competitors
- indemnities and D&O insurance available for directors.

When a person feels flattered to be asked to sit on a board, it may be difficult to make all of these inquiries. While the best approach is to be satisfied on all these points before accepting the appointment, the diligence exercise need not stop once the person is on the board. A director should continue to ask these questions in the course of becoming better acquainted with the corporation. If at any point a director regrets having accepted the board appointment, in light of what he or she has subsequently discovered about the corporation, that director should consider whether continued service on the board is appropriate.

LEAVING THE BOARD

There may come a time when a director wishes to step down from the board, for any one of a number of reasons. His or her other professional commitments may no longer leave enough time to devote to the corporation; personal circumstances may make it difficult for a director to continue to participate fully in the work of the board or the director may simply be ready for a change.

A director may also choose to leave the board because of a concern with the corporation. For example, if a director was not able to conduct thorough due diligence on the corporation before joining the board (as described above) and subsequently discovers matters about the corporation that make the director uncomfortable about being identified with the organization, that director may wish to step down at the first opportunity. If a director cannot support the CEO's vision for the corporation, it may not be appropriate to remain on the board. If the corporation is facing insolvency and a director is not confident about his or her ability to steer clear of significant personal liability, he or she should consider resigning.

There may be times when a director steps down at the corporation's initiative. Many corporations have a policy requiring directors to retire when they reach a certain age (often 70 or 72). In some cases the needs of the corporation may have changed and it may be in the corporation's best interests for certain directors to step down to make way for others with a different skill set or perspective. The challenge of course is for directors who are being asked to make way for others to regard this as a natural progression of the corporation's development and not as a personal slight.

When a director wishes (or is asked) to step down from the board, but is prepared to serve out the end of his or her term, the solution is simply not to allow his or her name to be put before the shareholders at the next annual meeting. A director's term in office is typically one year (although it can be as long as three years under most statutes). There is of course no legal reason that directors must serve out their terms. They are free to step down at any time by submitting a resignation in writing in accordance with the applicable corporate statutes (usually to the corporate secretary). In some cases, where there is a need to add a particular individual to the board between annual meetings, a sitting director may agree to tender his or her resignation in order to free up a place.

What should directors do if they feel they are being pushed off a board for asking too many questions, or when they leave the board voluntarily because they cannot support what the board and management are doing? Should a director go quietly or should he or she speak out? The answer, of course, depends entirely on the circumstances. However, directors should be aware that most corporate statutes provide them with a mechanism to make a statement to shareholders explaining why they are resigning or why they are opposed to being removed or replaced as a director. This is a powerful tool for directors, although it is seldom used. The director simply delivers the written statement to the corporation and the corporation either includes it in the information circular or delivers it separately to shareholders in advance of the meeting at which the director is to be removed from office or the director's replacement is to be elected.

WHAT DIRECTORS NEED TO KNOW – HIGHLIGHTS

Read the rest of this book. It is important. The following summary highlights some of the most important issues covered in these pages.

- Be thoughtful about the boards you join.
- Always act in a manner consistent with your fiduciary duty and duty of care.
- Understand the role that you play as a member of a board — usually your role will be to monitor how management is doing, not to manage the corporation yourself.
- Understand how the corporation's actions will affect not only the corporation's shareholders, but also its other stakeholders.
- Be confident that you have the right information on which to base your decisions.
- Receive the reports and recommendations of management and advisors with healthy scepticism — question the assumptions, analysis and conclusions until you are satisfied.
- Establish processes to analyze and make decisions that are independent of considerations other than the best interests of the corporation.
- Understand the statutory liabilities to which you are subject and how to exercise due diligence to do your job effectively and to avoid liability.
- Have indemnities and insurance in place that will fund your defence.
- Know when to leave the board.

PART II

How the Corporation Works

This part of the book explains how a corporation is created, the framework for accountability established in the corporate statutes, and the roles of the five main players in the governance process: the shareholders, the board of directors, management, the internal auditor and the external auditor.

CREATING A CORPORATION

A corporation is created by statute. A "business corporation" is a corporation with shareholders who have made an investment in the corporation's equity in the hope of earning a return on that investment. The shareholders typically earn this return when the corporation pays dividends on their shares or when they sell their shares (provided of course that their shares have increased in value).

A corporation's articles of incorporation (or a comparable document) together with the by-laws and any unanimous shareholder agreement (in the case of private companies) are often referred to as the corporation's "constating documents" or "charter documents". These documents, together with the legal requirements set out in the relevant statutes, form the framework of the corporation's governance. Securities laws and stock exchange listing rules impose certain additional corporate governance requirements on corporations that come under their jurisdiction. Best practices are the final piece. The TSX Guidelines, for example, set out 14 best practices recommended by the report of the Day committee, a private sector committee sponsored by the TSX.

BASIC CORPORATE MODEL

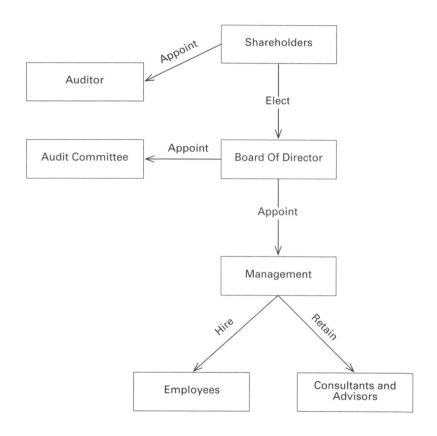

Business corporations are of course not the only form of corporate entity. Not-for-profit corporations are generally formed under a statute that provides for non-share capital corporations — in other words, the corporation has members rather than shareholders and the members are not entitled to the profits earned by the corporation. Public sector corporations, including Crown corporations, are typically created by special acts of parliament. While there are differences in the governance requirements set out in the statutes governing these entities, the basic governance principles are the same as those described in this book for business corporations.

Legal requirements prescribe a set of minimum standards, not a complete regime for effective governance. Notwithstanding the growing body of legal and regulatory requirements in the area of governance, a great deal is left up to the board and management. Understanding the policy reasons behind the legal requirements will help those involved in the governance process build on those requirements and establish governance practices appropriate to the corporation.

THE FRAMEWORK OF ACCOUNTABILITY

This chapter describes how each of the players in the governance process is put in place and how the financial reporting process operates to ultimately make the board of directors accountable to the shareholders.

The shareholders own the equity in the corporation but have no role in the operation of the corporation's business. They elect the directors, appoint the external auditors and approve certain specific types of transactions which could "fundamentally change" the nature of the corporation or its business. Otherwise, they have little say about the way in which the corporation operates.

The board of directors performs a "stewardship" function. It sees that the corporation's business is properly managed, in the first instance by appointing the CEO. The CEO in turn selects a management team (sometimes, but not always, with input from the board). Management hires employees and retains consultants and advisors and then operates the business throughout the year under the supervision of the board.

At the end of the year, management prepares annual financial statements setting out the results of the corporation's operations for the previous 12-month period and the financial status of the corporation at year-end, comparing those results with the results of the prior year. The board of directors reviews those statements and, when it is satisfied, approves the statements and delivers them to the shareholders. The delivery of the annual audited financial statements to the shareholders is timed so that the shareholders are in a position to review the statements before the annual meeting during which they elect directors for the next year. Once the shareholders have seen how the previous year turned out for the corporation from a financial perspective, they can determine whether to vote the same directors back into office or to replace the directors with other individuals in whom they have more confidence.

The shareholders also appoint outside auditors who are independent of the corporation. The outside auditors audit the annual financial statements prepared by management and express an opinion on those statements to the shareholders. This allows the shareholders to be confident about the integrity of information on which they are relying.

The other major player in the governance process is the internal auditor. Ideally, the internal auditor is appointed by and reports to the audit committee or the board of directors. In situations in which the internal auditor reports to management, directors should be sensitive to independence issues that may arise when the internal auditor is accountable to the very people whose controls it is reviewing.

At its most basic, this is the framework of accountability of Canadian corporations. There are a number of shortcomings inherent in this governance model, many of which are discussed in this book. The dynamic nature of governance thinking today is evidence of the significance that corporations and their stakeholders attach to corporate governance.

Claude Lamoureux's Eleven Point Speech

On March 4, 2002, Claude Lamoureux, President and Chief Executive Officer, Ontario Teachers' Pension Plan Board, addressed The Canadian Club of Toronto. In what has been referred to as the "Eleven Point Speech", Mr. Lamoureux outlined the changes for effective corporate governance:

> *The era of structural and cosmetic change is behind us. It's time to get serious about corporate governance and bring about change that matters.*
>
> *Simply put, institutional investors have to act forcefully in the best interests of Canadians on whose behalf they invest.*
>
> *Let me close with a summary of suggestions for institutional investors, corporations and governments.*
>
> *First, all fiduciaries should vote the shares they hold — and report on how they voted to those for whom they invest. This applies as much to mutual funds, banks and insurance companies as it does to pension funds.*
>
> *Second, corporations should be required to report the results of each shareholder vote within one day of the annual general meeting ... if not the same day.*
>
> *Third, governance committees should seek the active involvement of their institutional investors in recruiting independent directors.*
>
> *Fourth, all directors should invest their own money in the shares of companies they govern. Nothing aligns the director and shareholder interests quite like having your own money on the line.*
>
> *Fifth, the board should have regular sessions in the absence of management.*
>
> *Sixth, Canadian regulators should work with the CICA to promote the best accounting standards ... as opposed to the least offensive.*
>
> *Regulators should find independent individuals who are more than securities or financial specialists to oversee compliance.*
>
> *It is heartening to see an OSC panel reject a penalty for insider trading negotiated by staff.*
>
> *We need more common sense outrage and less clubby negotiation behind closed doors.*

Seventh, all press releases should be based on GAAP earnings or at least reconciled to GAAP earnings — and the releases should be approved by both the auditor and audit committee.

Eighth, annual reports, quarterly reports and proxy circulars should be written in clear language that makes sense to ordinary investors. Claims of sophistication and complexity are not an acceptable defence for obfuscation.

Ninth, auditors should not be allowed to earn other fees of any kind from the companies they audit.

Tenth, laws should be changed to make share ownership and options tax neutral.

And finally, the cost of options should be clearly charged on the P&L and disclosed in the financial statements and should be deducted from income.

THE SHAREHOLDERS

A business corporation allows shareholders to invest in a business undertaking without putting more at risk than the amount they paid for their shares. Whatever losses the corporation suffers, whatever liabilities it incurs, whatever damage it might do to someone else, the shareholders are not responsible to pay any further amounts. We often refer to the "corporate veil" which protects the shareholders from any liability for the actions of the corporation. While there have been cases where this veil has been "pierced" (i.e., a shareholder has been held liable for the actions of the corporation), this is difficult to do and has only happened in closely-held corporations.

One of the results of the link between a corporation's performance and its governance practices has been a more engaged and vocal investor community. Canada's institutional investors, in particular, have well developed perspectives on various governance issues and speak candidly about these issues with boards and management of the entities in which they invest. Their use of the rights and powers they have as shareholders has allowed them to influence the development and implementation of corporate governance practices.

Shareholders of Canadian corporations have a defined set of rights and powers. A very general overview of these rights and powers is set out here.

Canadian Coalition for Good Governance

In June 2002, a group that includes Canada's largest funds, pension funds, mutual funds and money managers formed the Canadian Coalition for Good Governance under the leadership of Claude Lamoureux, President and CEO, Ontario Teachers' Pension Plan Board and Stephen Jarislowsky, Chairman, Jarislowsky Fraser Limited. The members of the Coalition have agreed to share information and to take the initiative to hold management accountable for growing long-term shareholders value.

In April 2003, the Hon. Michael H. Wilson was elected as the first Chairman of the Coalition and Professor David R. Beatty became its first Managing Director.

The mission of the Coalition is to improve the performance of publicly traded corporations through the promotion of good governance practices across Canada. The Coalition plans, among other things, to develop and maintain an issues list of governance opportunities across "owned companies" (companies in which Coalition members have invested), to post the current status of those companies on the Coalition website and to publish a report annually on compliance with the Coalition's objections.

The Coalition's website is www.ccgg.ca.

Right to Elect Directors

Under most Canadian statutes, only the shareholders have the right to elect directors (a few jurisdictions, such as Alberta, permit creditors or employees to appoint directors under some circumstances). A shareholder who controls more than 50% of the votes at a shareholders' meeting is said to "control the board". This means that the share holder holds enough shares to carry the vote on who will be the directors. If the corporation is "widely held" (that is, if it has a large number of shareholders, none of whom owns a significant number of shares), then a person holding a substantial percentage, but less than the majority, of the shares is often able to control the board (because not all of the shareholders will attend the meeting or send in proxies).

Although every director must act in the best interests of the corporation rather than the interests of any particular shareholder, a shareholder who controls the board will typically exercise its voting power to elect as directors, individuals who see the world as it does.

BEST PRACTICE

Nominating committee

The TSX Guidelines recommend that the board of directors of every corporation appoint a committee of directors composed exclusively of outside (i.e., non-management), directors, a majority of whom are unrelated directors, with the responsibility for proposing to the full board new nominees to the board and for assessing directors on an ongoing basis.

Canada's institutional investors support the establishment of a nominating committee as contemplated in the TSX Guidelines, but will not withhold votes from a slate of directors simply because there was no such nominating committee, unless corporate performance over a suitable time frame is unsatisfactory. Ontario Municipal Employees Retirement Board proxy voting guidelines state that it will withhold votes from non-independent directors who are also members (or proposed members) of the audit, compensation, nominating or corporate governance committees of the board.

Voting by Proxy

In corporations that have more than a minimum number of shareholders, the right of shareholders to vote by proxy ensures that shareholders are not disenfranchised when they are unable to attend a meeting. Most corporate statutes require management to send a form of proxy to the shareholders prior to the meeting, together with an information circular (also called a proxy circular or management information circular), which must be approved by the board, containing the information necessary to enable shareholders to make an informed decision about the matters to come before the meeting.

Typically shareholders appoint a member of management to act as their proxy, but they are free to appoint another person. In the proxy itself, shareholders can give unlimited discretionary authority to the person they appoint as their proxy, or they may provide specific instructions to the proxyholder on how the shares are to be voted.

An information circular sent to shareholders in connection with a meeting at which directors will be elected will include a list of names of individuals which the corporation is proposing to the shareholders for election as directors (as well as certain information about these individuals). These nominees are referred to as the "management slate". The shareholders may vote either in favour of the management slate or they may withhold their vote — they do not vote against the slate.

Who determines the names that will appear on the management slate? This has been an issue of concern from a governance perspective for almost a decade in Canada. In many corporations, there was (and in some cases continues to be) a tradition of the CEO determining whose names should be put before the shareholders for election as directors. The concern with this practice is that directors may feel indebted for their position on the board to the CEO — the very person they are supposed to be supervising. It has therefore become a fundamental element of governance that directors who are independent of management determine who will be proposed to the shareholders for election as directors.

A person (usually a shareholder) who wishes to propose an alternative slate of directors is free to do so. Because this shareholder is "dissenting" from the slate proposed by management, it is referred to as a "dissident" or "dissident shareholder". In order to secure enough votes to have its own slate elected, the dissident shareholder will need to convince other shareholders to vote for its slate at the meeting or, ideally, to appoint it as their proxy. In most cases, the law will require the dissident shareholder to deliver an information circular to the shareholders whose votes the dissident shareholder is soliciting, setting out the same type of information that management was required to provide about the management slate. Preparing and distributing a dissident circular and then soliciting votes from other shareholders can be an expensive and time-consuming process.

The CBCA has recently been amended to make it easier for those who do not support management's recommendations to solicit proxies to vote to oppose those recommendations. A person may contact up to 15 shareholders to discuss how they will vote without sending a dissident's proxy circular. Proxies may also be solicited without sending a dissident proxy circular if the solicitation is done, for example, through newspaper or radio advertisements, provided that the advertisements contain certain prescribed information (such as the name of the shareholder soliciting the proxies, the percentage of the corporation's shares that shareholder holds and any interest the dissident shareholder has in the matter). The corporate statutes other than the CBCA do not yet permit proxies to be solicited in this way. Some provincial Securities Acts also regulate the solicitation of proxies.

CANADA'S INSTITUTIONAL INVESTORS

Proxy voting guidelines

Canada's institutional investors have had significant influence on the development of corporate governance practices. Among these are Canada Pension Plan Investment Board, Ontario Teachers' Pension Plan Board, Ontario Municipal Employees Retirement Board, and the Caisse de dépôt et placement du Québec. Each of these institutions has developed and published proxy voting guidelines, setting out how they intend to vote in respect of particular governance matters.

Representation of Minority Shareholders and Other Stakeholders
Minority shareholders often negotiate with the other shareholders for the right to nominate one or more of the members of the board. This is most common in privately held corporations, but can and does occur in public corporations. Stakeholders other than shareholders (such as lenders and labour unions) may also negotiate the right to appoint someone to the board. Having a seat at the board table will

give a minority shareholder (or other stakeholder) access to information presented to the board and with an opportunity to have their voices heard. Of course, all directors have a fiduciary duty to the corporation. To the extent that this duty conflicts with any obligation the director may feel to the stakeholder who put him or her on the board, the situation may become very uncomfortable for the director. The difficult position in which "nominee directors" find themselves is discussed in Part IV.

Cumulative voting

In most corporations, one person holding a majority of the shares cast at a meeting is able to determine who the directors will be. If directors are elected through "cumulative voting", each shareholder has the right to cast a number of votes equal to the number of voting shares it holds, multiplied by the number of directors to be elected. The shareholder may cast all such votes in favour of one candidate or distribute them among the candidates in any proportion it chooses. Under this system, it is possible for minority shareholders to elect one or more directors.

Most corporate statutes allow the corporation to adopt cumulative voting by amending its articles. The New Brunswick corporate statute mandates cumulative voting. In a number of cases in recent years, shareholders have made proposals to their fellow shareholders to adopt cumulative voting. These proposals generally argue that cumulative voting is a more democratic approach to electing directors and that it promotes the independence of the board from management. Opponents contend that directors elected by minority shareholders tend to be much more focused on the constituency they are seen to represent. Institutional shareholders (such as Teachers and OMERS) have not been prepared to support cumulative voting as a policy matter, but will consider supporting it in cases where it will ensure an independent voice on an otherwise unresponsive board of directors.

Right to Remove Directors

If the shareholders are unhappy with the way in which the corporation is being managed, their recourse is generally to replace the current directors with directors in whom they have more confidence. This can be done in one of two ways; the shareholders can wait until the end of the directors' term (which is usually one year) and then elect someone else in their place, or if the shareholders are so unhappy with one or more of the directors that they do not wish to wait until the end of their term before taking action, they can remove the director or directors from office. It is important to recognize that only shareholders can remove a director from office. It is often mistakenly thought the board can remove one of its own members — that is not the case. Shareholders can remove a director from office by passing an "ordinary resolution" doing so, which requires a majority of votes cast at the meeting called to remove that director. Calling a meeting to remove directors also requires significant time and resources.

Right to Appoint Auditors

The shareholders appoint the outside auditors to audit the financial statements and give them an opinion on those statements. Although it is clear that this power belongs to the shareholders under Canadian law, it is a bit different under American law. Under many of the U.S. corporate statutes there is no clear language about who appoints the auditors and accordingly the power is deemed to be vested in the board of directors. U.S. securities laws put U.S. public corporation shareholders in the same position as shareholders of both public and private corporations in Canada, by requiring that the name of the auditor be submitted to the shareholders for approval.

In public corporations (and in private corporations where there are more than a few shareholders) it is impractical for the shareholders to make their own determination about who the external auditor should be. The information circular, provided to the shareholders in connection with a shareholders meeting, proposes the name of the person for the shareholders to appoint as auditor. The shareholders appoint the auditor through an ordinary resolution (a majority of votes cast). Only shareholders have the power to remove the auditor. This is done by way of an extraordinary resolution (two-thirds of votes cast at a meeting).

If an auditor resigns, is being removed or is not proposed for re-election, there are extensive corporate and securities law requirements intended to alert shareholders to any conflict between the auditor and management that may have led to that result. Like directors who are being removed or replaced (see Part I), an auditor who is resigning, is being removed from office or who is not being reappointed is entitled to make a written statement to the shareholders. The auditor simply delivers the statement to the corporation and the corporation either includes it in the information circular, or delivers it separately to shareholders in advance of the meeting at which the auditor is to be removed from office or the auditor's replacement is to be appointed.°

Auditing and Assurance Standards Oversight Council

In October 2002, Canada's Chartered Accountants established the Auditing and Assurance Standards Oversight Council (the "AASOC") to over see the activities of the Assurance Standards Board (the "ASB"), with Jim Baillie as its first chair. The ASB is the national body with the authority and responsibility for setting auditing and assurance standards for the public and private sectors. In a press release announcing the members of the Council, the CICA described the ASSOC as follows:

> Reporting to the public and consisting of prominent leaders from business and regulators, it brings a broad perspective to complex issues facing standard setters, and supports the ASB in setting auditing and assurance standards in Canada and in contributing to the development of internationally accepted assurance standards. AASOC's responsibilities include appointing ASB members and providing input on strategic priorities. AASOC members, many of whom represent particular constituencies, including users, preparers of financial and other reports and auditors who provide assurance on these reports.

Right to Approve Certain Matters

For the most part, management and the board make decisions about the corporation and the direction it will follow and are not required to consult the shareholders. There are, however, certain matters which are considered "fundamental changes" in the life of the corporation which cannot be taken without shareholder approval. A number of these fundamental changes are quite technical and will not be of general interest for the readers of this book. The important thing to remember is that only specific types of actions require shareholder approval. Unless authority is specifically vested in the shareholders, the prerogative to take or approve any particular action rests with the board. The following is a list of the more common types of action which require shareholder approval:

- electing and removing directors;
- appointing and removing auditors;
- making changes to the corporation's articles or by-laws;
- amalgamating with another corporation (other than a parent, subsidiary or sister company);
- selling "all or substantially all" of the corporation's assets;
- entering into a plan of arrangement (one or more corporate steps or transactions that are impracticable to implement under the provisions of the statute and are therefore implemented pursuant to an order of the court); and
- dissolving the corporation.

Securities laws and stock exchange requirements also require shareholder approval of certain transactions which involve insiders. Very often, the approval threshold is set at a "majority of the minority" — in other words, the voting disregards the votes of the insider (such as the majority shareholder) who may have an interest in the transaction and only authorizes the transaction to proceed if a majority of the other shareholders (the "minority" in other words) approves the transaction.

The TSX requires that the shareholders approve certain transactions involving the issuance of shares, including transactions that may materially affect control of the corporation and transactions that have not been negotiated at arm's length. The TSX rules also require approval of certain stock option plans and share compensation arrangements. Particular rules apply to share compensation to insiders.

Right to See Certain Corporate Records
The shareholders have the right to examine the following corporate records (and take extracts of them) during normal business hours:
* the corporation's articles of incorporation;
* the by-laws, minutes of meetings of shareholders and resolutions of shareholders (but not of the board of directors or any of its committees, with certain exceptions);
* notices of any changes in the directors; and
* a copy of the securities register (showing all of the registered shareholders of the corporation).

Certain Other Rights
Shareholders have several other important rights, in particular the right to:
* requisition a meeting of shareholders (if the shareholder requisitioning the meeting holds not less than 5% of the voting shares);
* submit a proposal for consideration at a meeting of shareholders (if the shareholder holds the prescribed number of shares); and
* obtain a court order directing an investigation of the corporation.

The Right of Shareholders to Restrict Power of Directors
As discussed above, the division of power between the board and shareholders gives the power to manage the corporation to the board, leaving the shareholders with only limited rights of approval over very specific issues. However, the corporate statutes give the shareholders the opportunity to alter that balance of power. In some cases, this is done by putting restrictions on the authority of the board into the corporation's articles or by-laws. In other cases, the shareholders enter into a unanimous shareholder agreement. Each of these approaches is discussed below.

Restrictions in the Articles or By-Laws

The corporation's articles or by-laws may include restrictions in the following areas:

- the business the corporation may carry on and the power it may exercise
- issuance of shares
- repurchase of shares
- making, amending or repealing by-laws
- filling a vacancy on the board
- where the directors may meet
- participation in directors' meeting by phone (or other electronic means)
- quorum for a directors' meeting
- appointing officers, specifying their duties and delegating power to them
- setting remuneration for directors, officers and employees
- borrowing money or granting security.

Unanimous Shareholder Agreement

A "unanimous shareholder agreement" is an agreement between *all* of the corporation's shareholders (both voting and non-voting shareholders) that restricts some or all of the powers of the directors. This type of agreement enables the shareholders to exercise those powers themselves. For example, if the shareholders wish to limit the amount of money that the corporation borrows, they can take away from the board the power the board would otherwise have to authorize corporate borrowing. For a more detailed discussion, see Part VIII.

In some cases, the shareholders wish to take all of the powers away from the directors and exercise those powers themselves. A unanimous shareholder agreement having this effect is often put in place, for example, if a multinational company establishes a Canadian subsidiary through which it will carry on business in Canada. Like any corporation, the Canadian subsidiary will have one or more directors and those directors will be responsible for managing or supervising the management of the business and affairs of the corporation. Under most statutes, some of those directors must be resident Canadians and, accordingly, the board cannot be composed entirely of executives working out of the parent company's head office if a multinational wants to manage the business and affairs of the corporation itself (rather than leaving that responsibility with the board). It can put a unanimous shareholder agreement in place, stripping the board of all or some of its authority, and taking that authority for itself. A unanimous shareholder agreement may be put in place temporarily — even for the purpose of obtaining a single approval. This is often done when approvals must be obtained for transactions involving a corporate family and it is more practical to obtain the signature of a wholly-owned subsidiary's parent than the signatures of all of the subsidiary's directors.

Unanimous shareholder agreements are often used in private companies. It is common, for example, for minority shareholders in a private corporation to require, as a condition of investing, that certain corporate actions not be taken without their approval. Where the right to approve these actions would otherwise be within the exclusive purview of the board, the requirement that the approval of some or all of the shareholders be obtained will be set out in a unanimous shareholder agreement.

A unanimous shareholder agreement (as defined by statutes and discussed above) often includes additional provisions that do not restrict the directors' powers, but deal with other matters. There is sometimes confusion about the difference between unanimous shareholder agreements and shareholder agreements generally. "Shareholder agreement" is not really a technical term — it can apply to any agreement between some or all of the shareholders. A shareholder agreement will typically deal with a variety of matters between shareholders — how the shares will be voted and when the shareholders will be entitled to sell their shares, and to whom, for example. Only if all of the shareholders sign an agreement can it validly restrict the powers of the directors. Often, however, the entire document will be entitled a "unanimous shareholder agreement", even though many of its provisions do not restrict the powers of the directors and would be equally effective if contained in an agreement between only some of the shareholders. Similarly, a document called a "shareholder agreement" often includes a unanimous shareholder agreement as well as a number of other provisions.

ENHANCED GOVERNANCE MODEL

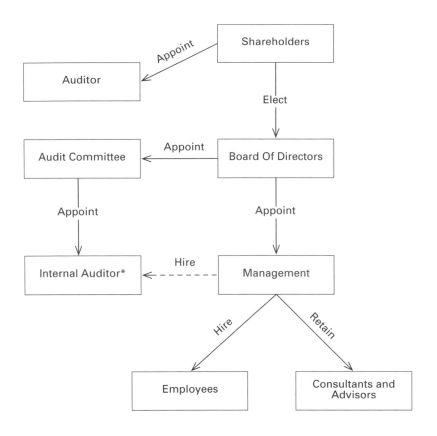

*The relationship between the internal auditor and the Audit Committee and/or management is discussed in Part II.

THE BOARD OF DIRECTORS

Managing vs. Supervising Management

The board of directors of the corporation is responsible for *managing or supervising the management of the business and affairs of the corporation*. In small private companies the shareholders often serve as the directors and officers as well. However, in most corporations of any size (and certainly in public companies), a professional management group runs the business under the supervision of a board of directors. The board selects the CEO to head up the management team, approves the direction in which management proposes to lead the corporation and then monitors the way in which the CEO and his or her team performs. Usually the board becomes more actively involved only if the corporation faces certain challenges, such as a take-over bid, financial instability or charges of illegal or improper activities.

Who makes the decision about how involved the board will be in the management of the corporation and its business? Practically speaking, the functions of the board and management result from the styles and personalities of the individuals who comprise the board and the management team as well as the challenges which the corporation faces over time. In a public company, there is an expectation that the board will hire and supervise a professional management team. If a public company board becomes very involved in day-to-day activities, it may suggest a lack of confidence in management. At the end of the day, however, the ultimate responsibility for managing rests with the board and it is the board that determines how "involved" it should be in management.

BEST PRACTICE

NACD on director professionalism

The report of the NACD's Blue Ribbon Commission on Director Professionalism (2001 Edition) recommends that board responsibilities include the following:
- Approving a corporate philosophy and mission.

- Selecting, monitoring, evaluating, compensating and, if necessary, replacing the CEO and other senior executives, and ensuring management succession.
- Reviewing and approving management's strategic and business plans, including developing a depth of knowledge of the business being served, understanding and questioning the assumptions upon which such plans are based, and reaching an independent judgment as to the probability that the plans can be realized.
- Reviewing and approving the corporation's financial objectives, plans and actions, including significant capital allocations and expenditures.
- Reviewing and approving material transactions not in the ordinary course of business.
- Monitoring corporate performance against the strategic and business plans, including overseeing the operating results on a regular basis to evaluate whether the business is being properly managed.
- Ensuring ethical behaviour and compliance with laws and regulations, auditing and accounting principles, and the corporation's own governing documents.
- Assessing its own effectiveness in fulfilling these and other board responsibilities.
- Performing such other functions as are prescribed by law, or assigned to the board in the corporation's governing documents.

What Does It Mean to Supervise Management?

The challenge for most boards and their management teams is to understand what "supervising" or "monitoring" means. What should the board of directors be involved in and how detailed should their analysis be on any given issue? How does a board exercise oversight without infringing on the CEO's prerogative to make management decisions?

The line between "monitor" and "manage" is not always easy to discern. The NACD has coined the term "NIFO" (nose in, fingers out) to describe the role that directors should play. Although the board will typically leave day-to-day decisions to management, the monitoring function requires that the board reserve to itself the ability to intervene in management's decisions and to exercise final judgment on any matter which is material to the corporation. To be able to do this, the board must be satisfied that it is receiving reports regularly on matters significant to the corporation. It must review these reports thoughtfully, question management until the directors are satisfied with the responses, and retain outside advisors as necessary.

Criticism of board oversight

The appropriate exercise of oversight became an issue in and continues to be an area of focus as the details of other major corporate failures in the United States are revealed.

The report of the special committee of the board of directors of Enron (known as the "Powers Report") reads in part as follows:

> *The Board, and in particular the Audit and Compliance Committee, has the duty of ultimate oversight over the Company's financial reporting. While the primary responsibility for the financial reporting abuses discussed in the Report lies with Management, the participating members of this Committee believe those abuses could and should have been prevented or detected at an earlier time had the Board been more aggressive and vigilant.*

The Permanent Subcommittee on Investigations of the Committee on Governmental Affairs of the United States Senate held hearings into the collapse of Enron and issued a report, which included the following as its first finding:

> *The Enron Board of Directors failed to safeguard Enron shareholders and contributed to the collapse of the seventh largest public company in the United States, by allowing Enron to engage in high risk accounting, inappropriate conflict of interest transactions, extensive undisclosed off-the-books activities, and excessive executive compensation. The Board witnessed numerous indications of questionable practices by Enron management over several years, but chose to ignore them to the detriment of Enron shareholders, employees and business associates.*

Limitations on the Board's Right to Delegate

Although the board delegates much of its authority to management with respect to the operation of the corporation's business, corporate law prohibits the board from delegating certain specific functions. The list of these functions will vary from statute to statute. However, under the CBCA, the board may not delegate the following responsibilities to management or even to a committee of the board — these responsibilities must be discharged by the full board:

- issuing securities;
- declaring dividends;
- purchasing or acquiring shares of the corporation;
- approving the annual audited financial statements;
- approving an information circular delivered in connection with a solicitation of proxies;
- approving take-over bids and directors' circulars; and
- adopting, amending, or repealing by-laws.

BEST PRACTICE
_____

Saucier Report on the role of the board

The Saucier Committee identified the following responsibilities for the board in its report issued in 2001:
- Choosing the CEO and ensuring that the senior management team is sound, focused and capable of successfully managing the company.
- Setting the broad parameters within which the management team operates; examples include:
  - adopting a strategic planning process and approving a strategic direction
  - defining a framework to monitor the management of business opportunities and risks
  - in defined circumstances, approving corporate decisions
  - approving a communications policy that includes a framework for investor relations and a public disclosure policy which may involve a process for monitoring the relationship between the corporation and investment dealers.

- Coaching the CEO and the management team; the metaphor of a coach is chosen deliberately to underscore that the directors are not players — they should provide direction and advice, but they don't do management's job.
- Monitoring and assessing the performance of the CEO, setting the CEO's compensation and approving the compensation of senior management and taking remedial action where warranted, including replacing the CEO if necessary.
- Providing assurance to shareholders and stakeholders about the integrity of the corporation's reported financial performance.

MANAGEMENT

The corporate statutes allow the board of directors to appoint management (referred to as officers in the corporate statutes) and delegate to management virtually all of the power and authority of the board, subject to certain restrictions (see above). The board's responsibility is to satisfy itself that the delegation is appropriate and to monitor management's exercise of the delegated authority. Current governance best practice standards recommend that there be a clear delineation between the responsibilities of the board and the responsibilities of management and that this delineation be set out in formal position descriptions of the responsibilities of the board and of the CEO. These position descriptions go beyond the description of particular officer responsibilities often included in corporate by-laws. While more and more public companies are adopting this practice, most still operate on the basis of implied delegation. In other words, there may be no formal delegation of responsibility from the board to the CEO; the CEO is appointed and then goes about doing what CEOs customarily do, returning to the board for approval of certain actions when it is customary or appropriate to do so. The question, of course, is what is customary or appropriate. This will be interpreted differently by different boards and different CEOs in different circumstances.

Canadian Council of Chief Executives

Governance, values and competitiveness – a commitment to leadership

The Canadian Council of Chief Executives is composed of the chief executives of 150 Canadian corporations. Its corporate governance initiative, co-chaired by its chairman, Charles Baillie, and its chief executive officer, Thomas d'Acquino, was launched in July 2002. The report resulting from this initiative, *Governance, Values and Competitiveness — A Commitment to Leadership* sets out the consensus view of the Council's members on principles of corporate governance. It argues against the rules-based approach to corporate governance adopted in Sarbanes-Oxley and by the NYSE and Nasdaq in their proposed corporate governance listing standards, in favour of private sector initiatives to restore public confidence in business.

The recommendations set out in this report draw on established best practices and legislation and regulations adopted or being proposed in the United States. Among other things, the report recommends that chief executive officers provide a certification of quarterly and annual financial statements comparable to what is required under Sarbanes-Oxley.

The CCCE's website is www.ceocouncil.ca.

Because the CEO is actively engaged in the business on a daily basis and the outside directors have a more intermittent relationship with the corporation, the sense of a reporting relationship between the CEO and the board sometimes fades. Some CEOs take action without getting the appropriate board approvals and make important disclosures to the board on an information only basis. It is, of course, up to the board to resist this development and insist that it be as involved as it thinks appropriate in order to discharge its oversight function.

Position descriptions of a board and CEO

Position descriptions for the board and management are recommended as a matter of best practice in order to draw the line between "manage" and "monitor" and to ensure that management is reporting to and seeking approval from the board as appropriate. Guideline 11 of the TSX Guidelines states:

> *11. The board of directors, together with the CEO, should develop position descriptions for the board and for the CEO, involving the definition of the limits to management's responsibilities. In addition, the board should approve or develop the corporate objectives which the CEO is responsible for meeting.*

THE EXTERNAL AUDITOR

The financial statements are the most important information that shareholders receive about the corporation in which they have invested. The corporate statutes require that the statements be prepared in accordance with Canadian generally accepted accounting principles (referred to as "GAAP"). GAAP is a compilation of principles from which corporate accounting policies are selected and judgments applied. They also require (subject to certain exceptions) that the annual financial statements be accompanied by the report of an auditor who is independent of the corporation, its affiliates and the officers and directors of the corporation and its affiliates.

Role of the Auditor

The shareholders appoint the auditor each year. The auditor provides the shareholder with its opinion on the financial statements prepared by management — specifically whether they present fairly, in all material respects, the financial position of the company as at the date of the balance sheets and the results of its operations and its cash flows for the years indicated in accordance with GAAP. In order to give its opinion, the auditor performs an audit in accordance with generally accepted auditing standards (referred to as "GAAS"). GAAS sets standards about the auditor's qualifications, the performance of the auditor's examination and the preparation of the auditor's report.

The auditor works closely with management in the course of the audit and will meet regularly with the audit committee of the board. The audit committee will not typically recommend that the board approve the annual financial statements unless it knows that the auditor is prepared to issue its opinion. The auditor in turn typically will not issue its opinion unless it has a representation letter from management and knows that the audit committee is prepared to recommend that the board approve the financial statements and that the board is in fact prepared to approve these statements. This is to ensure that any knowledge the board and management both have, which is relevant to the financial statements, is properly reflected in those statements.

Appointment of Auditor

The influence of management on the reappointment of auditors has been central to the issue of auditor independence. The concern is whether the auditor can be critical of management in performing its audit and provide an objective opinion on those statements (or be perceived as doing so) if it knows that management will have a direct influence on whether they are reappointed. Responsibility for selecting the person to be put before the shareholders should therefore rest with the board of directors, based on a recommendation from the audit committee (or entirely with the audit committee). The audit committee will of course seek input from management, but should be able to assess whether there have been any differences between management and the auditor which might colour management's endorsement of the incumbent auditor for the following year.

U.S. stock exchanges require that the audit committee "charter" (also referred to as a "mandate" or "terms of reference") specify that the audit committee and board of directors have the ultimate authority and responsibility to select, evaluate, and where appropriate, replace the auditor (or to nominate the auditor to be proposed for shareholder approval in any proxy statement). Under Canadian law, it is clear that it is the shareholders who appoint the auditor. For

Canadian companies there is no specific requirement to include a reference to this in the charter, but more and more companies are doing so, both as a reminder of the auditor's accountability to the shareholders and to stay current with U.S. standards. The Saucier Report recommended that the audit committee charter explicitly affirm that the board of directors and the audit committee (as representatives of the shareholders) have the ultimate authority and responsibility to select, evaluate, and where appropriate, recommend replacement of the external auditor. This is, of course, subject to the right of shareholders to appoint and remove the auditor.

RECENT DEVELOPMENTS

Accounting oversight board

In 2002, the Canadian Public Accountability Board was established as an independent organization to oversee auditors of public companies. Former Bank of Canada Governor Gordon Thiessen is the chair of the CPAB's Council of Governors.

The mission of the CPAB is to contribute to public confidence in the integrity of financial reporting of Canadian public companies by promoting high quality, independent auditing. The members of the board of the CPAB will oversee the design, implementation and enforcement of a system of independent inspection of auditors of Canada's public companies. The CPAB will report annually to the public on the conduct of its activities and results achieved.

The CPAB was in the process of filling the remaining board positions before proceeding with its mandate.

Consulting Services Provided by the Auditor

Often an auditor (and the auditor's affiliates) provides services to the corporation in addition to audit services. The corporate families to which auditors belong offer a variety of financial and other consulting services. Although other consultants and financial advisors (including competing accounting firms) may offer the services and expertise comparable to those offered by the auditor's firm, it may be most cost effective for the issuer to retain the auditor because of the auditor's expertise and familiarity with the corporation and its business. However, the importance of auditor independence outweighs cost effectiveness in today's governance environment.

When a member of the auditor's corporate family performs non-audit services for the corporation, there is a potential for conflict (or at least the perception of conflict) in at least two areas that should be addressed by the audit committee. First, the auditor should not be auditing his or her own work. For example, if the auditor (or an affiliate) has provided consulting services in an area critical to the financial reporting system, the audit committee should ask whether the auditor can be independent in its assessment of systems which it was responsible for creating and implementing. If the auditor has provided tax-planning advice, the audit committee should question whether the auditor can be objective in the presentation of financial results if that presentation may be critical of or affect the tax planning.

Second, since it is management that typically retains consultants, the audit committee should concern itself with whether the auditor's interest in obtaining the consulting work influences how critically it reviews the financial statements prepared by management.

The audit committee must understand the nature of any and all relationships between the auditor and the corporation (in addition to the audit relationship) and satisfy itself that these relationships do not compromise the independence of the auditor in conducting the audit. The best practice standard (driven in part by requirements in the United States) is for audit committees to pre-approve non-audit engagements between the external auditor and the corporation. In many cases, the audit committee establishes a threshold, below which pre-approval is not necessary, but requires that even minor non-audit engagements be reported to the audit committee.

Independence standards – CICA exposure draft

The independence of the external auditor has been an issue of considerable focus, particularly in the United States. In 2000, the SEC introduced certain restrictions on the non-audit services which an external auditor could provide. In 2002, the Public Interest and Integrity Committee of the Canadian Institute of Chartered Accountants ("CICA") proposed new Canadian independence standards for auditors and other assurance providers. These standards are intended to be consistent with U.S. restrictions and are subject to change when the full extent of the provisions of Sarbanes-Oxley are known.

The Exposure Draft proposes that the external auditor be prohibited from providing the services set out below:

- financial statement preparation services and bookkeeping services to an audit client that is a listed entity, except in emergency situations;
- valuation services where the valuation involves matters that are material to the financial statements that will be subject to audit or review and the valuation involves a significant degree of subjectivity;
- actuarial services to an audit client that is a listed entity that provides insurance services, unless the company uses its own actuaries to provide management with its primary actuarial services;
- internal audit services to an audit client that is a listed entity that has over $50 million in total assets (US$200 million in the U.S.), where the internal audit services represent more than 40% of the internal audit activities for the particular entity;
- designing or implementing a hardware or software system for an audit client that is a listed entity unless management takes full responsibility for all aspects of the project;
- legal services to an audit client that is a listed entity where the results of the service will be material to the financial statements;
- certain recruiting services that create an unacceptable self-interest, familiarity or intimidation threat for an audit client that is a listed entity; and
- certain corporate finance activities that create an unacceptable advocacy or self-review threat.

THE INTERNAL AUDITOR

The internal audit function reviews various aspects of the conduct of an organization's operations and reports on what it has found. As a profession, internal auditors are governed by the Institute of Internal Auditors, which describes internal auditing as an "...independent, objective assurance and consulting activity designed to add value and improve an organization's operations. It helps an organization accomplish its objectives by bringing a systematic, disciplined approach to evaluate and improve the effectiveness of risk management, control, and governance processes."

The internal auditor is typically an employee of the organization on which it reports, although in some organizations, the internal audit function is outsourced (i.e., the company hires an outside consultant to perform the internal audit function). In order to maintain the independence of the internal audit team, the best practice is for the internal audit group to remain separate from the rest of the organization and for the head of internal audit not to be part of the management team. The independence of the internal auditor is further strengthened where hiring, compensation, and performance reviews are the responsibility of the audit committee and that the internal auditors operates under a mandate approved by the audit committee. Under this model, the head of internal audit is appointed by and reports to the audit committee, with a dotted line relationship only to a senior member of management (preferably the CEO and in any case not the CFO). The internal auditor will still have a relationship with management for administrative matters (for example, human resource matters relating to the internal auditor's employment relationship) but will report to the audit committee.

Not all companies have a formal internal audit function. In corporations that do not, the board should consider how, in the absence of that function, management and the board satisfy themselves that the corporation's risk management, control and governance processes are operating effectively. There has been considerable debate about whether the external auditor should be permitted to provide internal audit services. At the root of this controversy is a concern that the external auditor not be auditing its own work and a concern that it not be involved in making management decisions.

NYSE requirement for an internal audit function

The internal audit function has been the subject of increasing focus as companies, regulators and legislators seek to improve corporate governance practices. The proposed amendments to the NYSE's corporate governance listing requirements provide that every NYSE listed company have an internal audit function. The commentary to this proposed requirement states:

> This requirement does not necessarily mean that a company must establish a separate internal audit department or dedicate employees to the task on a full-time basis; it is enough for a company to have in place an appropriate control process for reviewing and approving its internal transactions and accounting. A company may choose to outsource this function to a firm other than its independent auditor.

REPORTING TO THE SHAREHOLDERS

All corporations must report certain basic financial information to their shareholders. The nature of the information the corporation must provide to its shareholders changes after the corporation has more than a small number of shareholders (that number is 15 under the CBCA, for example) and then again if the corporation issues securities to the public. Each of these three levels of disclosure is discussed in more detail below.

Basic Disclosure Applicable to All Corporations

Under most statutes, a corporation is required to hold an annual meeting of shareholders and to deliver to its shareholders a notice of such meeting and the audited annual financial statements. The process for approving and delivering these statements is discussed above.

Additional Disclosure for Corporations with More Than a Small Number of Shareholders

Corporations with more than a small number of shareholders must allow the shareholders to vote by proxy and must provide them with a form of proxy for this purpose. The corporation must also send a management proxy circular (referred to as an information circular or proxy circular in some statutes) containing prescribed information. The disclosure in the circular relating to the annual meeting must include:

- the names of shareholders holding more than 10% of the voting shares;
- the number of voting securities held by each person nominated for election as a director;
- details of any financial assistance given to shareholders, directors, officers, employees and certain other persons (if the financial assistance was material to the corporation);
- particulars of any indebtedness of the directors and officers to the corporation; and
- information on the interests of insiders (which includes 10% shareholders, directors and officers) in material transactions.

It also includes executive compensation disclosure and disclosure of amounts paid to directors.

Additional Disclosure for Public Companies

Public companies (referred to as "reporting issuers" in some provinces for securities law purposes) must disclose certain information each year. Some of this information must be delivered to shareholders. Other information must be filed with the securities regulators, who make that information publicly available, generally on a website called "SEDAR" (the System for Electronic Analysis and Retrieval) maintained by the securities regulators (www.sedar.com).

Public companies must:

- deliver to their shareholders (and file with the regulators) audited annual financial statements and unaudited quarterly statements, accompanied by a narrative discussion of those statements referred to as MD&A (management's discussion and analysis of financial condition and results of operation); the MD&A must include a description of any known trends or uncertainties that affect (or the corporation thinks will affect) the results of continuing operations;

- deliver the information circular described in Chapter 13 above, in connection with any meeting of the shareholders;
- file an annual information form (AIF) with securities regulators each year; the AIF is intended to provide background information on the corporation necessary to understand the nature of the corporation, its operations and prospects; it includes a history and description of the business, financial information, information about the capital structure and the market for the corporation's securities as well as information about the directors and officers; and
- issue a press release whenever a "material change" occurs and, in some provinces, file a material change report with the securities commission; insiders of the corporation must file reports about any trades in securities of the corporation.

Finally, the TSX require listed corporations incorporated in a Canadian jurisdiction to include a Statement of Corporate Governance Practices, either in the information circular delivered to shareholders in connection with the annual meeting or in the corporation's annual report. This disclosure must include a complete description of the corporation's system of governance, with specific reference to each of the TSX Guidelines. Where the corporation's system is different from any of those guidelines (or where the guidelines do not apply to the corporation's system) the disclosure must include an explanation of the differences or inapplicability. The TSX has recently proposed amendments to these guidelines which are expected to be released by the OSC for public comment shortly.

FRAMEWORK FOR FINANCIAL REPORTING

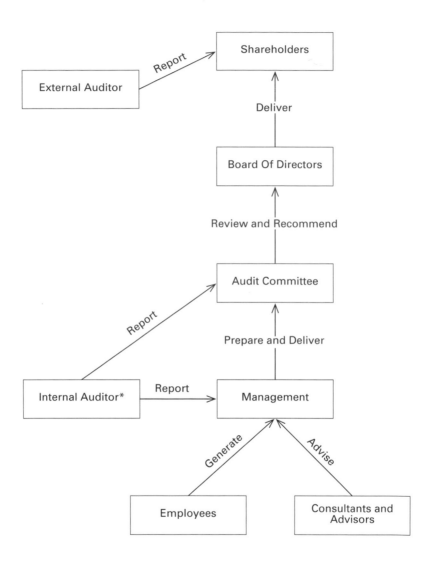

PART III

How the Board Works

This part of the book discusses how the board is set-up and how it functions.

CONSTITUTION OF THE BOARD

Who Sits on the Board

Generally there are three categories of directors:

- members of management (and those with a close relationship with management),
- representatives of particular shareholders (or other stakeholders), and
- independent directors.

The process for selecting and putting forward the names of candidates for election to the board is discussed in Part II.

The composition of the board will depend in part on whether the corporation is public or private and which stock exchange it is listed on (if any). It is customary for the chief executive officer to sit on the board (although it is not required). In some cases, one or more other members of management may also sit on the board. Smaller public companies often have additional members of management and their close advisors (such as outside counsel or financial advisors) on the board, at least in part because of the challenge of attracting truly arm's length outside directors to the board. These advisors are not generally seen as being independent of management. Significant shareholders (or their representatives) may wish to sit on the board or to nominate candidates with whom they have a close relationship. The rest of the board will be made up of independent directors, that is, directors who have no relationship with management or any significant shareholder. In private companies, there is often less emphasis on independent directors. The founders or members of the family of the original founder will typically have the strongest representation on the board.

Many Canadian corporate statutes require that a certain percentage of the directors be "resident Canadians". Most require that a majority of the directors be resident Canadian. The CBCA recently reduced this requirement to 25% of the directors.

Number of Directors
The number of directors on the board will depend on the size of the corporation and the complexity of its business, and on whether it is a private company or has public shareholders. Most statutes require public companies to have at least three directors, while private companies may have just one director. Beyond that, a company may have as many or as few directors as it wishes. The company's articles will set out how many directors the corporation has (or a minimum and maximum number of directors it may have, with the determination of the exact number of directors left with either the shareholders or the board).

The challenge is for the board to be large enough to have the right balance of skills and experience represented, but not so large that it becomes difficult for each director to contribute effectively. For most Canadian public companies, a board comprised of between five and 16 directors is usually appropriate. The TSX Guidelines encourage boards to consider their size with a view to ensuring that they are able to function effectively, although reducing the size of boards is a less significant issue today than it was 10 years ago when large companies (such as the banks) had 40 or more directors.

Term in Office
Directors typically serve for a term of one year and stand for re-election at each annual meeting of shareholders. Most statutes permit directors to serve for terms of up to three years.

Staggered boards

In some companies, part of the board will be elected at one annual meeting for a term of two years and the rest of the board will be elected at the next annual meeting, again for a term of two years (or a third of the board may be elected annually, each for a three-year term). These boards are referred to as "classified" or "staggered" boards.

If a company has a classified or staggered board, the entire board will never come up for re-election at the same time. Proponents of this approach argue that it results in greater continuity of the board. Critics argue that shareholders are less able to change a board they are unhappy with.

Teachers' has the following comments on classified or staggered boards:

> We see many disadvantages with a classified system. Staggered terms for board members make it more difficult for shareholders to make fundamental changes to the composition and behaviour of boards, by making it extremely difficult for any challenge to, or change in, board control. In circumstances of deteriorating corporate performance, this difficulty could result in a permanent impairment of long-term shareholder value.
>
> We prefer the annual election of all directors. We will generally NOT SUPPORT proposals that provide for staggered terms for board member
>
> When a proposal to adopt staggered terms for directors has been approved by a vote of shareholders, we will generally SUPPORT the directors who are standing for staggered terms in those instances in which a vote for such directors is viewed to be in the financial interest of the shareholders and in conformity with the guidelines for the election of directors. We do not believe it is appropriate to vote against such directors simply as an indication of disagreement with the manner in which directors are elected.

Importance of Independence

The independence of the board from management is one of the leading themes in corporate governance. The importance attached to director independence has developed from the conviction that directors who have no relationship with management and who do not owe their positions on the board to management are best able to monitor management's performance and to intervene when it is in the best interests of the corporation to do so.

Several categories of directors with at least an apparent independence from management or a particular stakeholder have been established in various Canadian statutes, regulations and reports. These categories include:

- outside directors
- unrelated directors
- independent directors.

Each of these definitions of independence is described in greater detail below. However, the real key to independence lies not in how it is defined, but in how the director behaves. A director who meets the applicable definition of independence may not in fact function independently of management. In some cases this may be a question of temperament — a "don't rock the boat" approach to the role as a director. In other cases, it may reflect a relationship with management that is not caught by the applicable definition, but which nevertheless interferes with the director's ability to be critical of management and its decisions.

CURRENT ISSUE

Director remuneration

Director remuneration is an issue that is attracting more and more attention in Canada — not that directors are paid too much, but that they are paid too little. Directors of many sizeable publicly traded companies in Canada receive an annual retainer of as little as $15,000 a year, with an additional payment (also referred to as a "per diem") for each meeting the director attends of approximately $1,000. In light of the experience and expertise most directors bring to the corporations they serve, the time it takes for directors to discharge their duties properly and ever increasing exposure to personal liability, this is clearly inadequate. It also pales in comparison to the amounts paid to directors in other jurisdictions, particularly the United States. This makes it difficult for Canadian companies to attract directors from outside of Canada. Some institutional shareholders are starting to speak out on the need to pay directors amounts commensurate with the responsibilities they assume.

Director compensation is set by the board itself — shareholder approval is not required. Public companies must, however, disclose to their shareholders every year the compensation paid to directors, including any amount which directors earned from the corporation as consultants or experts.

In February 2003, the CPP Investment Board released its Proxy Voting Principles and Guidelines. These guidelines state that the CPP Investment Board will oppose stock options for directors, for executives and for employees. With respect to director stock options it states:

> We do not support the granting of share options to directors. This form of compensation is inferior to direct share ownership and has the potential to misalign the financial interests of directors with those of shareholders.

With respect to stock options for management and employees:

> We do not support the granting of stock options to management or employees. Stock options are problematic in many areas, including their effectiveness in aligning management interests with those of the shareholders, the potential dilutive impact on existing shareholders, their tendency to focus management on short-term performance, their use as a cash incentive rather than an ownership incentive, and intractable accounting issues. While many aspects of granting stock options could be improved, the result in our view would still be inferior to direct share ownership.

Approaches to Defining Independence

There are two general approaches to defining "independence". The first is to leave it up to the board of directors to determine what constitutes independence for that corporation. This is the approach currently used in the TSX Guidelines. The second is to establish "bright line" tests—certain relationships that will disqualify an individual from being considered "independent", such as being employed by a "material service provider". Usually these two approaches are combined. The board is ultimately responsible for determining whether a director is independent. A statute or stock exchange requirement may require them to presume that individuals with certain current or past relationships with the corporation are not independent. The various tests of independence are described below.

RECENT DEVELOPMENTS
_____

Cooling-off periods

In an effort to enhance board independence (and the perception of that independence), proposed amendments have been made to the corporate governance listing requirements for the NYSE, Nasdaq and the TSX. All propose certain "cooling-off periods" for individuals who have had relationships with the corporation. A "cooling-off period" is a period of time which must have elapsed after that relationship with the corporation has ended before that individual can be considered "independent" or "unrelated" for the purposes of the applicable listing requirements.

Each of these exchanges has a different approach to who will be subject to cooling-off periods and the applicable period of time.

The proposed NYSE amendments would impose five-year cooling-off periods for:

- certain employees of the issuer (those receiving $100,000 a year or more in direct compensation);
- employees and affiliates of the issuer's auditor;
- employees of another company that has an executive officer of the listed company on its compensation committee;

- certain suppliers and customers (where the corporation accounts for the greater of 2% or $1 million of the supplier's gross revenue or where the customer accounts for the greater of 2% or $1 million of the corporation's gross revenue); and
- directors with immediate family members in any of the foregoing categories.

The NYSE is recommending a transition rule pursuant to which this required presumption will not apply unless these thresholds were exceeded after the date or which this history standard came into effect.

The proposed Nasdaq amendments would impose three-year cooling-off periods for:
- employees;
- a director who accepts (or who has a non-employee family member who accepts) payments from the issuer in excess of $60,000 (subject to certain exceptions, such as directors' fees);
- a director who has an immediate family member who is an executive officer of the corporation;
- a director who is a partner, controlling shareholder or executive officer of any non-profit organization which received payments from the company that exceeded 5% of the non-profit's revenues or $200,000 (whichever is larger);
- a director who is employed as an executive officer of another entity where any of the company's executives serve on the compensation committee of the other entity; and
- a director who was a partner or employee of the company's outside auditor and worked on the audit.

The proposed TSX Amendments would impose three-year cooling-off periods for:
- officers and employees of the issuer; and
- material service providers of the issuer.

Outside Directors/Unaffiliated Directors

Most Canadian corporate statutes require some of the directors to be "outside directors". The CBCA, for example, requires that a public company have at least two outside directors. Outside directors are directors who are not employees or officers of the corporation or its affiliates, and are referred to as outside directors because they are seen to be "outside" of the management of the corporation. "Inside directors" are of course part of the management group of the organization.

This distinction between inside and outside directors has been in the corporate statutes for many years and is quite outdated. These concepts do not address many of the possible relationships between a director and management which could create issues of independence. In addition, it is important to note that, because a controlling shareholder is an "affiliate" of the corporation, its officers and employees are considered "inside directors". Most of the more modern definitions of independence do not preclude directors from being considered independent if their only relationship with the corporation relates to shareholding. Unlike most other definitions of independence, however, controlling shareholders are excluded from the corporate law concept of "outside" directors. The exception is Sarbanes-Oxley, which does not consider an "affiliate" to be independent for the purposes of audit committee composition.

Federal financial institutions legislation (such as the *Bank Act*) uses the term "unaffiliated director", a term that captures many more relationships which could affect, or be perceived to affect, a director's judgment than does the definition of "outside director". It includes, for example, a significant borrower of the bank and a major supplier of goods and services to the bank. Financial institutions legislation generally requires that at least two-thirds of the directors of banks and trust companies be "unaffiliated". It is intended to identify those directors who are, or are perceived to be, at arm's length from the corporation's business, its management, or any other person with an interest in a matter affecting a corporation.

Unrelated Directors

The concept of "unrelated director" comes from the TSX Guidelines, which define an unrelated director as follows:

> An unrelated director is a director who is independent of management and is free from any interest and any business or other relationship which could, or could reasonably be perceived to, materially interfere with the director's ability to act with a view to the best interests of the corporation, other than interests and relationships arising from shareholding.

The TSX Guidelines recommend as a matter of best practice that a majority of every board of directors be unrelated, to ensure that the board functions independently of management.

RECENT DEVELOPMENTS

Definition of "unrelated director" in TSX guidelines

The TSX has recently submitted proposed amendments to its corporate governance listing requirements to the OSC. Although it will continue to be a best practice guideline that a board be composed of a majority of unrelated directors, the TSX proposes to introduce as a condition of continued listing that a company have at least two unrelated directors.

In addition, the TSX proposes to amend the definition of "unrelated director" as follows:

> *"unrelated director" means a director who is: (a) not a member of management and is free from any interest and any business, family or other relationship which could reasonably be perceived to materially interfere with the director's ability to act with a view to the best interests of the issuer, other than interests and relationships arising solely from holdings in the issuer (b) not currently, or has not been within the last three years, an officer, employee of or material service provider to the issuer or any of its subsidiaries or affiliates and*

(c) not a director (or similarly situated individual) officer, employee or significant shareholder of an entity that has a material business relationship with the issuer. TSX does not consider a chair or vice chair of the board of directors who is not a member of management to be a related director.

This proposed new definition clarifies certain aspects of the existing definition by stating that a member of management is not an unrelated director and that the chair and vice chair of the board who are not members of management are not related directors. It also introduces two new "bright line" tests. Officers, employees and "material service providers" cannot be considered unrelated for a period of three years after that relationship ends (this is often referred to as a "cooling-off period"). In addition, directors, officers, employees and significant shareholders of an entity that has a material business relationship with the issuer are not unrelated.

Independent Directors

Although reference is often made to "independent directors", that term only occurs in a statutory or regulatory context in Canada in the OSC's Rule 61-501 and its Quebec counterpart QSC 27. Rule 61-501 deals principally with transactions related to sales and purchases of the corporation's shares, such as insider bids, issuer bids, going private transactions and related party transactions. It recommends (and only in restricted circumstances requires) transactions of this nature to be reviewed by a special committee of directors who are independent for the purpose of the transaction. To be considered "independent" for the purposes of a particular transaction, one must be able to conclude that there are no adverse factors which affect or could be perceived as affecting the director's decisions or actions on the matter. Adverse factors would include:

- employment and professional relationships with the corporation, or other parties to the transaction over the preceding 12-month period;
- any material financial interest in the transaction; and

- any benefit (financial or otherwise) expected to be received as a consequence of the transaction that is not being received by all other shareholders on the same basis.

Board independence

Canada's institutional investors place a great deal of emphasis on the independence of the board. They each have their own definition of "independence", which builds on the TSX definition of "unrelated" to give specific examples of individuals whom they would not consider to be independent (such as relatives of members of management and persons who receive consulting fees from the corporation (such as lawyers and investment and commercial bankers)).

Both Teachers and OMERS specifically state in their proxy voting guidelines that they will not vote against a slate of directors simply because it fails to meet the independence standards, unless corporate performance is unsatisfactory.

Developments in the United States

In the post-Enron era, there is probably no single issue that receives more focus in the United States than the issue of director independence. There has been a movement away from allowing the board to make its own determination in favour of establishing bright line tests. These bright line tests preclude a board in most cases from concluding that individuals with certain relationships with the corporation can be considered independent of management. The term "independent" is used in Sarbanes-Oxley in the context of members of the audit committee and by the NYSE and Nasdaq both in the context of the composition of the board and the compensation, governance and audit committees of the board.

Corporate governance requirements for smaller issuers

One of the debates in Canada is over whether smaller companies should be subject to the same corporate governance requirements as larger issuers. On September 17, 2002, Linda Hohol, President of the TSX Ventures Exchange, wrote to David Brown in response to his August 15, 2002 open letter seeking input on the appropriate Canadian response to Sarbanes-Oxley.

Ms. Hohol makes the arguments for not imposing on junior issuers (i.e., those listed on the TSX Ventures Exchange) the same corporate governance requirements as senior issuers (i.e., those listed on the TSX):

> *Although junior and senior issuers are subject to generally similar regulatory requirements, there are certain differences as to business, structure and Exchange oversight applicable to more junior issuers that we wish to highlight. We believe that these differences have a significant impact on the corporate governance practices that should be applied to these issuers.*
>
> *The focus of the issuer's business is squarely concentrated on operations. Such issuers do not have complicated structures, multiple divisions or numerous employees. In fact, the average size of a junior issuer board of directors is approximately five, with the majority having expertise in the specific industry of the issuer. Funding for these issuers is always an issue, and resources are generally not expended on items that are not related to the actual operation of the business.*
>
> *These issuers cannot be viewed in the same context as senior issuers that possess significantly larger and more complex corporate and financial structures and very different business models and objectives. As a result of their operation focused mandate, junior issuers do not possess the degree of corporate sophistication as their more senior counterparts. As such, the Exchange's regulatory model for our issuers is quite different from that of more senior exchanges. Whereas the boards of more senior listed issuers are able to manage the operations and*

undertake transactions with minimal exchange oversight, the Exchange Regulations significantly limit our issuers' management discretion both in respect of corporate structure and transaction terms. Exchange Regulations govern virtually all scenarios where securities or a significant amount of cash will be issued or expended by issuers. Exchange

Regulations frequently involve a review of significant transactions prior to their being undertaken by issuers to ensure that they meet the standards established by the Exchange. Such a review, we believe, is much more far reaching in this regard than the provisions in the Sarbanes-Oxley Act and the NYSE Requirements.

Following from this analysis, Ms. Hohol then argues that a number of the changes to corporate governance regulation and best practices should not be applicable to junior issuers. For example, she argues that there is no need for TSX Ventures listed companies to have more than two independent directors. This, she says, is due to several factors, including the small average board size of junior issuers, the constraints imposed on the actions of the issuers by the Exchange Regulations and the fact that there is a relatively small pool of potential directors available to junior issuers.

COMMITTEES

General

Boards (particularly public company boards) discharge many of their responsibilities through committees. There are two reasons to delegate a particular area or issue to a committee. First, it is often more effective for a smaller group of directors to turn their minds to a particular matter. Second, a committee of the board can be constituted to ensure the independence of the process. Management is typically excluded from the audit committee, for example.

Composition of Committee

Audit committees must have a specified number of outside directors. The TSX Guidelines currently recommend that the audit committee be composed only of outside directors and that other committees of the board (such as the compensation committee and governance committee) be composed entirely of outside directors, a majority of whom are unrelated directors. If a statute requires that a certain percentage of directors be resident Canadians, that statute will typically also require that the same percentage of the members of any committee be resident Canadians (although this requirement was recently removed from the CBCA).

Composition of board committees and the definition of independence for this purpose is in a state of flux at the moment. By the end of 2003 these concepts will largely be settled both in Canada and in the United States.

Which Committees are Required?

Public companies are required to have an audit committee. This requirement appears in the corporate law, although Canadian securities regulators and stock exchanges are in the process of introducing requirements that all public entities (or listed companies in the case of the TSX) have an audit committee. It is very common for public companies to have compensation committees and nominating/governance committees. Depending on the size of the company and the industry in which it operates, its board may have a variety of other committees, including committees responsible for oversight of environmental matters, occupational health and safety, risk management and finance. These are all "standing committees" of the board.

CURRENT ISSUE

Requirement to have an audit committee

In May 2002, the Five Year Review Committee (appointed by the Minister of Finance to review securities legislation in Canada) released its draft report, recommending regulatory action in a number of areas related to corporate governance. Among them was a recommendation that every listed entity be required to have an audit committee:

There has been a strong preference in Canada not to legislate corporate governance practices beyond what is currently provided in the corporate statutes. The prevailing view has been that best practice guidelines, coupled with disclosure requirements, would drive most issuers towards best practices that were most appropriate for them. However, in light of the importance of the financial reporting process to the integrity of an issuer's financial statements and the regulatory force of audit committee standards in the United States, it is appropriate today to look for a means of establishing a common standard in this area and enforcing compliance with that standard.

As we mentioned at the outset, the requirement for audit committees had its genesis in corporate law statutes. However, we believe that all reporting issuers should have audit committees and audit committees in Ontario should all operate to the same standard. Accordingly, we support legislative amendments that would provide the Commission with rulemaking authority relating to the functioning and responsibilities of audit committees. Moreover, we think it is also important that reporting issuers in all Canadian jurisdictions hold their audit committees to a consistent standard. Accordingly, we encourage the other CSA jurisdictions to provide their Commissions with similar powers and for the CSA to work together on an expedited basis to establish standards for audit committees that will place Canadian audit committees in the "best of class" internationally.

Other than the few legal requirements referred to above, there have been relatively few restrictions and guidelines relating to the composition and mandate of board committees until recently. Concern with board independence and diligence in several key areas has led to requirements being imposed on audit committees under Sarbanes-Oxley and to proposals by the CSA, TSX, NYSE and Nasdaq.

Special Committees
In addition to standing committees of the board (such as audit, compensation and nominating/governance committees), boards may establish special committees from time to time to deal with specific issues. For example, if the corporation proposes to enter into a transaction with a major shareholder, it is often advisable for it to

establish a special committee of directors unrelated to the significant shareholder to consider the transaction and make recommendations to the board. If the corporation faces a crisis, such as a particularly serious piece of litigation, it may also be advisable for the board to establish a special committee of directors to devote the additional time necessary to focus on that issue.

Authority of Committees

Committees only have the authority delegated to them by the board. While it is possible for the board to delegate the authority to make decisions to a committee (subject to certain restrictions discussed in Part II), it is more common for committees to make recommendations to the board and for the board to make the final decisions, based on the recommendations of the committee. If the board does delegate authority to a committee, it is not relieved of its responsibility with respect to the matters within the committee's mandate — it must continue to exercise the same oversight that it does when it delegates authority to management. If the committee makes recommendations to the board, the board must review the reports and recommendations of the committee as it would any other input it receives, ask the pertinent questions and make any further inquiries necessary to make an informed business judgment.

LEADING DECISION

Audit committee – Standard Trust decision

The OSC decision in Standard Trust is discussed below. Much of the OSC's discussion in that decision focused on the audit committee and the role it played in the events leading up to the release of inaccurate financial statements. The OSC had the following comments about the performance of the audit committee:

The members of the audit committees bore somewhat more responsibility than the other directors for what occurred at the July 24 directors' meetings because they had a greater opportunity to obtain knowledge about and to examine the affairs of the companies than the non-members had and,

BOARD COMMITTEES

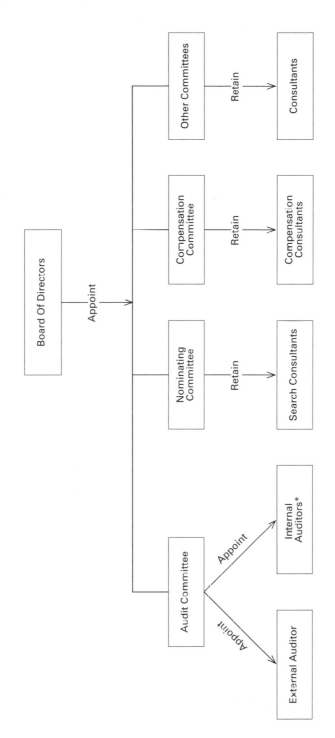

*The relationship between the internal auditor and the Audit Committee and/or management is discussed in Part II.

consequently, more was expected of them in respect of overseeing the financial reporting process and warning other directors about problems.

Re Standard Trustco Ltd. (1992), 6 B.L.R. (2d) 241 (O.S.C.)

HOW THE BOARD MAKES DECISIONS

Formulating the Board's Decision

Directors function collectively as a body, referred to as the "board of directors". Unless specific authority is delegated to an individual director by the board, he or she has no authority to cause the corporation to take any action or to bind the corporation in any way. Most boards strive to make decisions by consensus rather than putting resolutions to a vote.

Every member of the board of directors is equal, at least in law. If this legal theory does not always survive in practice, it is not because any one director has more power or authority in fact than the others, but because certain directors dominate the board. No director can dominate without the acquiescence of the others, but it seems to be human nature for members of any group to defer to those they perceive to be more knowledgeable about an issue (such as directors who are members of management), who have a greater stake in the corporation (such as a major shareholder) or who enjoy greater seniority.

Fettering the Discretion of the Board Not Permitted

Directors must be free to exercise their discretion, unfettered by obligations to or directions from others, including shareholders. Directors may not, for example, agree that they will make a particular decision as some other person may direct.

Directors May Not Vote by Proxy

Individual directors are not permitted to delegate their authority to any other person. They may not, for example, give their proxy to another person and ask them to act on their behalf at a board meeting. This is different from the rights of shareholders, who are entitled to vote by proxy. Board decision making is a question of business judgment exercised in the best interests of the corporation. The corporation is entitled to the benefit of the judgment of those individuals the shareholders have elected as directors.

U.S. requirements for certain committees

The proposed amendments to the New York Stock Exchange listing requirements will require listed companies to have not only an audit committee, but also a nominating/governance committee and a compensation committee (or committees with other names, but with the same responsibilities). These committees will be required to have a written charter which includes specified responsibilities.

MEETINGS

Meetings in Person
As discussed above, directors do not have any authority individually (unless authority has been specifically delegated to them by the board). They can only act as members of the board of directors. This model contemplates directors meeting to discuss issues of concern to the corporation and formulating a board decision. In order for the corporation to have the full benefit of the judgment and experience of the directors elected by its shareholders, all directors must present at the meeting and engage in full and frank discussion of the matters before them. While this is not always possible or practical, directors should strive to meet this standard as often as possible.

Participation by Phone
Directors will usually be entitled to participate in meetings by phone, although this is not desirable in most cases. It is difficult for directors who are connected by phone to hear everything that is being said — and certainly impossible for them to appreciate the body language

and other visual cues. The director who is participating by phone may also have difficulty having his or her perspective heard and may not be fully engaged in the meeting.

There will, of course, be situations in which it is better for the board or committee to have one or more directors participate in the meeting by phone, rather than losing the benefit of their participation altogether. Boards should, however, resist having this become a regular practice.

Resolutions in Writing

Many statutes permit the board to approve a particular action by having all of the directors sign a resolution. This is often appropriate when the board must formally approve a matter that has previously come before the board. Generally, however, it is better practice for the directors to meet in person so that they may engage in full and frank discussions about matters of concern to the corporation.

In Camera Meetings

In camera meetings of the board are meetings, or portions of meetings, that exclude certain individuals. Most common are *in camera* meetings of outside directors—that is, meetings that exclude members of management (even if they are also directors) and *in camera* meetings of independent (or unrelated directors)—that is meetings that exclude directors who do not qualify as independent (or unrelated). This provides an opportunity for discussions which may be difficult with all directors present in the room. It may also be appropriate from time to time for outside or independent directors of the board to meet privately with particular members of management or with outside advisors. Committees of the board also hold *in camera* sessions of their meetings. For example, the audit committee should meet with each of the external auditor and internal auditor separately, in both cases without management present.

KEEPING NOTES AND CORPORATE RECORDS

Notes can be a double-edged sword. It is often prudent for there to be only one record of the deliberations of the board of directors — the minutes which are approved by the board and inserted with the company's corporate records. It may create problems if the official record is subsequently challenged by conflicting notes kept by individual directors. Accordingly, the company's corporate secretary will often suggest that directors keep their own notes, if they wish, until the minutes have been approved and then destroy them.

On the other hand, directors should remember that while action is taken by the board as a whole, directors may incur liability on an individual basis. Accordingly, it may be important for individual directors to be able to prove that they raised certain objections or were unaware of a particular course of conduct being proposed by the company's management or by its controlling shareholder. Directors who do not have their own records of critical situations may find themselves unable to establish their due diligence defence.

Notwithstanding the value to individual directors of their own notes if they need to prove their version of a particular set of events, directors should also recognize that, if litigation arises, it is unlikely that they will be able to keep those notes private. They will be asked on discovery whether they kept notes of the situation under scrutiny and will probably be required to produce them. In these circumstances, some directors — and their board colleagues — have deeply regretted the existence of those notes. References to issues which were of concern to a director — and which the director did not pursue — could well be damaging to the director individually or to the board as a whole. Notes indicating a director's privately held assessment of board colleagues or members of management inevitably prove embarrassing if they become public.

The practice among directors to either keep or discard their notes varies. However, it is prudent for all directors to insist that the formal minutes kept of a meeting record anything that is necessary for a director to establish a due diligence defence. For example, if a board is relying on the advice of outside advisors or on the company's audited financial statements, this fact should be recorded in the minutes. If a statutory test must be met before a particular action may be taken (for example, a solvency test in the case of the payment of dividends), the board's consideration of this test should be recorded. If a director disagrees with a particular course of action and is not content to have the record imply a consensus on the matter, that director's dissent should be shown in the minutes. This is, of course, particularly important if personal liability flows from the particular course of action.

THE CHAIR

The role of the chair is critical to the effective functioning of the board. The specific powers and responsibilities of a chair will depend on a number of factors, including whether the chair is also the CEO, whether there is a controlling shareholder, and the independence and style of the other directors on the board. As a general matter, however, the chair is responsible for setting the agenda for meetings of the board, ensuring that the directors receive the information they need in order to operate effectively at the board meeting and for chairing meetings of the board.

The role of the chair is much more than an administrative function. The chair sets the tone for the relationship between the board and management. He or she will often play a significant role in the development of the corporation's strategic direction and may act as a spokesperson for the company in its relationships with shareholders and other stakeholders.

The separation of the positions of chair and CEO has been one of the most controversial issues in the Canadian governance debate. Both the Dey Committee and the Saucier Committee initially recommended the separation of these two positions, but under pressure from the business community, softened their recommendations. There is no legal requirement that these positions be separate and even the TSX Guidelines refer only to the need for independence in board structures — stopping well short of recommending that these positions be separated as a matter of best practice.

Higgs Report on role of the chair

Review of the Role and Effectiveness of Non-Executive Directors (referred to as the "Higgs Report") was released in the United Kingdom in January 2003. It recommends that the board chair assume the following responsibilities:

The Role of the Chairman
The chairman is responsible for:

* leadership of the board, ensuring its effectiveness on all aspects of its role and setting its agenda;
* ensuring the provision of accurate, timely and clear information to directors;
* ensuring effective communication with shareholders;
* arranging the regular evaluation of the performance of the board, its committees and individual directors; and
* facilitating the effective contribution of non-executive directors and ensuring constructive relations between executive and non-executive directors.

Separation of Chair and CEO

There is no legal requirement that these positions be separate and even the TSX Guidelines refer only to the need for independence in board structures — stopping well short of recommending that these positions be separated as a matter of best practice. The TSX Guideline states:

> 12. *Every board of directors should have in place appropriate structures and procedures to ensure that the board can function independently of management. An appropriate structure would be to (i) appoint a chair of the board who is not a member of management with responsibility to ensure the board discharges its responsibilities or (ii) adopt alternate means such as assigning this responsibility to a committee of the board or to a director, sometimes referred to as the "lead director". Appropriate*

procedures may involve the board meeting on a regular basis without management present or may involve expressly assigning the responsibility for administering the board's relationship to management to a committee of the board.

No amendments to this guideline are currently being proposed. However, institutional investors generally advocate the separation of the positions of Chair and CEO. The following is an excerpt from the Ontario Teachers' Pension Plan Board Proxy Voting Guidelines:

The Chief Executive Officer, or CEO, is responsible for the day-to-day operations and management of the company. The Chair of the Board is responsible for co-ordinating the activities of the board, which, in turn, is responsible for evaluating the performance of the company and its CEO. We believe that these responsibilities put a combined Chair/CEO in the very difficult position of co-ordinating the body that is responsible for evaluating his or her own performance. We are also concerned that in these situations too much power or control may reside in one individual.

For these reasons we believe it is appropriate, in most instances, to separate the roles of CEO and Chair. We feel there is a great potential advantage to the corporation, the CEO, and the directors to have a separate Chair, who can deal with matters from the board's point of view, and who can provide a greater measure of independence to the board's oversight role.

In situations where the same person holds the Chair and CEO titles, we advocate the practice of appointing a "Lead Director" for the board. We note, however, that any standard description of the role and responsibilities of a Lead Director is almost indistinguishable from the role and responsibilities of an independent and non-executive Chair.

We will not ordinarily vote against a slate of directors where there does not exist a separation of board and management roles. We will do so if corporate performance, over a suitable time frame, is unsatisfactory.

THE LEAD DIRECTOR

When the CEO also acts as chair, many consider it desirable to appoint a "lead director" from among the members of the board. A lead director is an independent director who speaks for and provides leadership to the other independent members of the board. Often the lead director is the chair of the corporate governance committee (if there is one), but there is certainly no need for this to be the case. The lead director will typically chair *in camera* meetings of the independent directors and deal with the CEO on issues which the independent directors are reticent to raise with the CEO directly.

The concept of a lead director re-emerges each time attention focuses on the independence of the board. It was recommended in the Dey Report and is referred to in the TSX Guidelines as one means of promoting the independence of the board from management. The Saucier Report recommended that every board have an "independent board leader" who would: provide leadership to enhance board effectiveness (for example by ensuring that it has the appropriate resources); manage the board (including by setting the board agenda, in consultation with the CEO); act as a liaison between the board and management; and represent the corporation to external groups such as shareholders and other stakeholders at the request of the CEO.

GENERAL COUNSEL

Most companies face a range of complex laws, regulations, contractual obligations and other legal restrictions and requirements. Failing to deal with these matters effectively may not only create problems which are time consuming, difficult to unwind, and cause significant liabilities, but could also result in serious civil and criminal violations of law for the corporation, its officers and directors.

The board and management need to rely on expert legal advice to support many of their discussions and actions. In most corporations this advice is provided in the first instance by an internal legal officer with the title "General Counsel" (also referred to as "corporate counsel", "in-house counsel" or "inside counsel"). The general counsel is typically a generalist with a good business background and good legal instincts about the corporation's business. He or she will have an intimate knowledge of the corporation's history, ongoing activities and current challenges. The general counsel and his or her in-house legal team will understand the business and structure of the corporation and its various divisions, subsidiaries and affiliates and legal issues affecting the corporation on a day-to-day basis.

The general counsel typically reports to the chief executive officer but may in some larger organizations report to a very senior officer such as the chief operating or chief administrative officer. Where legal issues are a significant component of the corporation's risk profile (e.g., the corporation operates in a litigious environment or a highly regulated industry) the general counsel will usually report to the president or the chief executive officer. It should be noted, however, that the client of the general counsel and the in-house legal staff is the corporation and not the chief executive officer or other officer to whom the general counsel reports. The general counsel can provide the board with factual information about the corporation and its activities and expert legal advice that is based on a thorough hands-on knowledge and understanding of the corporation and its business both past and present. This continuity of knowledge and legal advice from past events, for the present activities and to the consideration of future actions is a vital component of the board's actions and understanding of the issues when "due diligence" or "all reasonable care" is the required standard.

The general counsel and the other in-house lawyers are responsible for legal compliance. They keep employees, officers and directors up-to-date on legal requirements and those affecting the aspects of the corporation's operations for which they are responsible. They arrange education and training for those who require it and generally oversee the corporation's compliance with statutory and regulatory requirements to which it is subject. The general counsel evaluates actual and contingent liabilities that he or she is aware of (often with the assistance of outside advisors) and provides other members of senior management and the board with his or her assessment of those liabilities.

The corporation will often retain or engage an outside law firm or firms for advice and expertise in specialized matters. In some cases the outside firm may also act as the "general counsel" for the corporation if the corporation does not have an in-house counsel. Specialized matters, including tax issues, competition and anti-trust matters, publicly issued or traded securities, patent, trademark and intellectual property matters, litigation (civil and criminal), mergers, acquisitions and divestitures, and civil and criminal investigations and trials, are often delegated to outside law firms which have specialists in these areas. The board should be aware of the relationships the corporation has with its outside law firms and the matters in which they are representing the corporation, even though such law firms are engaged, directed and managed by the general counsel or otherwise report only to the general counsel or another officer such as the CEO. The board should also hear directly from such law firms (in addition to the general counsel) when major transactions or material issues are involved and especially when the corporation is facing a crisis or is involved in a complex and high risk problem or legal issue. The board may also consider engaging another law firm to report solely to the board if a second opinion is needed or if circumstances otherwise warrant.

The general counsel can be and should be a valuable resource to the board of directors. The general counsel can assist the board in anticipating and dealing with legal implications of various courses of action by the board or the corporation. The general counsel can also advise the board and the directors about matters that may result in liabilities for the individual directors. The general counsel is in a unique position to provide the board with a continuity of knowledge and experience as well as legal advice and direction.

RECENT DEVELOPMENTS

Chief governance officer

More and more public companies in the United States are establishing the executive position of "chief governance officer"— among them Tyco International Ltd., Walt Disney Co., and Pfizer Inc. Chief governance officers are often, but not always, lawyers and are usually a senior vice president or equivalent level. The positions cross over the financial, compliance and investor relations functions and work closely both with other members of senior management and with the board.

CORPORATE SECRETARY

The corporate knowledge and specialized expertise of a corporate secretary is also an important resource for the board. The corporate secretary is responsible for organizing board meetings that have been called and for ensuring that the board has been provided with the necessary pre-board meeting materials. The corporate secretary must ensure that pre-board meeting materials are sufficient and concise enough to adequately describe all the issues, but not so voluminous that the directors are not able to read or digest the materials. The corporate secretary is also typically responsible for keeping the minutes of meetings and other important corporate records. The issues relating to record keeping are discussed in this part and in Part IV.

The corporate secretary function is often combined with the position of general counsel. As with the general counsel position, it is sometimes performed by outside legal counsel. In some larger organizations, the position of corporate secretary is a full-time position separate from that of the general counsel, especially in the case of public companies.

The corporate secretary plays an important role in the functioning of the board of directors, but is also an important part of the corporation's management team. In some organizations, where the CEO and the chair of the board positions are separate, the corporate secretary reports on administrative matters (such as corporate filings) to the chief executive or financial officer, but to the chair on matters relating to the board. In other cases the corporate secretary reports to the president or CEO and has a dotted-line responsibility to the chair of the board.

PART IV

Standards of Performance

EVERY DIRECTOR IS SUBJECT TO TWO BASIC DUTIES

Every director has two basic duties to the corporation — a fiduciary duty and a duty of care. These are very powerful concepts in law. A court will deal harshly with a director who has acted in a manner contrary to one or both of these duties, but will be very reluctant to question the decisions made by a board in a manner consistent with these duties. The deference of the courts to the decisions of an independent board which has followed a diligent process is referred to as the "business judgment rule" and it is described in more detail below.

It is important to understand that the fiduciary duty and duty of care are duties of each individual director. The theory is that if each director adheres to the appropriate standards of loyalty and care, board decisions which are properly motivated and appropriately thoughtful will follow. Because each individual director is required to act in accordance with his or her fiduciary duty and duty of care, regardless of what other members of the board might do, it is entirely possible for one director to have acted in a manner consistent with his or her fiduciary duty (or duty of care) with respect to a particular issue and for another to have breached that duty. The actions of the director who has breached that duty will attract liability, but the actions of the director who acted in a manner consistent with that duty will not. The fiduciary duty are described in detail below.

FIDUCIARY DUTY

A director's fiduciary duty is the cornerstone of his or her relationship with the corporation. The fiduciary duty is sometimes referred to as the duty of loyalty, although it involves much more than that. It requires the director to act honestly, in good faith, and with a view to the best interests of the corporation. For most directors this will seem intuitive; how else would they behave?

There are more opportunities for a director to run afoul of this duty than one might think. The fiduciary duty brings with it an obligation to prefer the interests of the corporation to those of any other person (including the very shareholder who was responsible for placing the director on the board to begin with). It also prevents the director from disclosing confidential information about the corporation and obliges the director to share certain information with the corporation.

The ramifications for a director of breaching his or her fiduciary duty are significant. The director can be sued by the corporation (or by certain other parties on behalf of the corporation) for any damage the breach of that duty caused. The corporation will be prohibited under most corporate statutes from indemnifying the director for legal and other costs if a director breached his or her fiduciary duty. Most statutes also prohibit the corporation from taking out insurance for the benefit of the director against liability relating to the director's breach of fiduciary duty.

Meaning of Fiduciary Duty

A fiduciary relationship implies vulnerability and dependency on the part of the beneficiary (in this case the corporation) and an ability on the part of the fiduciary (in this case the directors) to exercise discretion. The law imposes high standards of conduct on fiduciaries and deals with breaches of the fiduciary duty harshly. The legal impetus for characterizing the director's relationship with the corporation as being fiduciary in nature stems from the need for a corporation's stakeholders to be confident that the members of its board and management team will not manipulate the corporation for their own benefit. Without that confidence, the concept of the corporation as a separate legal entity which acts in its own best interests would have no credibility with shareholders, prospective investors or other stakeholders.

The fiduciary duty is set out in the corporate statutes as a requirement that directors *act honestly and in good faith with a view to the best interests of the corporation.*

Again, it is important to note that the fiduciary duty is imposed on every director (and officer) and it is therefore the responsibility of each director individually to ensure that he or she is acting honestly and in good faith with a view to the best interests of the corporation, regardless of how fellow directors may conduct themselves.

Conflict of Interest

It is not unusual for well-intentioned, honest directors to find that their own interests are different from the interests of the corporation and from a legal perspective that they may even conflict. This may happen, for example, if another company in which they own shares does business with the corporation.

To understand the law relating to director conflicts of interest, a director must understand that the common law (principles developed by the courts) prohibits directors from doing business with the corporation they serve. This is important because it is likely, if a director does not comply with the requirements of the corporate statutes in dealing with a conflict of interest, the director (and the contract or transaction in question) will be subject to the very stringent requirements of the common law.

The next step is to understand how the corporate statutes have modified this prohibition in certain cases, provided that the director makes the required disclosure about the conflict of interest, refrains from voting in most circumstances and provided above all, that the contract or transaction in question was fair and reasonable from the corporation's perspective.

Common Law Prohibition on Directors Doing Business with the Corporation

The common law prohibits directors from having any interest in a contract or transaction to which the corporation is a party. Although this is extremely restrictive, it has the advantage of avoiding any potential for a director to have divided loyalties.

At common law, the consequences of a director having any personal interest in a contract with the corporation are quite significant. First, the corporation is entitled to subsequently disavow the agreement, whether or not the director has profited from it. If the director has made any profit, the corporation is also entitled to require the director to pay that profit over to it. These rights may be enforced by the corporation directly or by certain other stakeholders pursuant to a derivative action (see Part VII).

Statutory Provisions Dealing with Conflict of Interest

The drafters of the corporate statutes recognized that a complete prohibition of the corporation doing business with a director or any entity in which a director has an interest is impractical and has the potential to create real problems. For example, it can preclude the corporation from doing business with key customers, suppliers and service providers (or from having individuals connected with customers, suppliers or service providers serving on the board). It can also make it difficult for the corporation to attract to its board individuals who have the knowledge and experience which would be useful to the corporation, because they will not want to put themselves in a position of not being able to do business with the corporation. To address these issues, most of the corporate statutes provide a procedure for the director to follow which will allow the corporation to enter into contracts in which the director has an interest without any of the negative consequences which the courts historically imposed, provided that the deal is fair to the corporation.

The procedure for dealing with conflicts of interest is quite technical and must be followed carefully in order to ensure that interested directors can shelter under its protection. The regime will apply if:

- the director does business with the corporation directly;
- the director is an officer or director of an entity that does business with the corporation; or

- the director has a material interest in an entity that does business with the corporation.

Directors must be careful to comply with the detailed requirements involved in these provisions. The first step is for a director to consult with legal counsel if there is any doubt as to the appropriate course of conduct. The following is a summary of the requirements in many of the corporate statutes:

- **Written Notice.** The director must notify the corporation in writing of his or her interest, generally at the time when the corporation (or the director) first becomes interested in the transaction. In some cases, the statute permits the directors to give a general notice of all entities in which they are officers and directors or have a material interest, stating that they should be regarded as interested in any contract or transaction with that entity. Directors seldom do this, although it is a good practice.
- **Abstain from Voting.** The second step is for the director to abstain from voting on any resolution to approve the contract or transaction in question (although he or she may be counted as part of the quorum). There are certain exceptions to this rule in most statutes. For example, the directors with an interest in the contract may vote on contracts with affiliates of the corporation. They may also vote on their own remuneration, indemnities in their favour from the corporation and on director's and officer's insurance.
- **Fair and Reasonable.** The final consideration is whether the contract or transaction was fair and reasonable to the corporation at the time it was approved or confirmed.

Under certain statutes it is possible to "cleanse" the transaction by having the shareholders ratify it. Under these statutes, even if the director did not adhere to the requirements relating to disclosure and abstention from voting, the contract or transaction will not be invalid and the director will not be accountable if three conditions are met:

- **Special Resolution of the Shareholders.** The shareholders approve or confirm the transactions by special resolution (two-thirds of votes cast).
- **Disclosure to the Shareholders.** Disclosure of the interest is made to shareholders in a manner sufficient to indicate its nature before the shareholders are asked to approve it.
- **Fair and Reasonable.** The contract or transaction was fair and reasonable to the corporation when it was approved or confirmed.

Appropriation of Corporate Opportunity

Directors are precluded from taking for themselves (or "appropriating") an opportunity about which they learned through their relationship with the corporation, if the corporation might want to pursue that opportunity. For example, if the corporation is considering an investment in a particular business, directors may not use the knowledge of that opportunity acquired as a result of their relationship with the corporation to take that opportunity away from the corporation and make the investment themselves.

The concept of "appropriation of corporate opportunity" developed from 19th century trust law, which insisted on unimpeachable conduct on the part of a trustee dealing with trust assets. A director is a fiduciary of the corporation just as a trustee is a fiduciary of the trust. Corporate opportunity is different from conflict of interest — there is no procedure for a director to follow to be able to appropriate a corporate opportunity with impunity. Typically, the courts will order a fiduciary to pay over to (or "account for") the corporation all profits realized as a result of the appropriated corporate opportunity. The courts have held directors to a very high standard in this area.

The difficulty for most directors is to determine when a "corporate opportunity" exists. The concept is not so broad that every vague notion that is floated in the executive offices of a corporation is regarded as a "corporate opportunity". Some courts have extended the protection to opportunities which they have referred to as having advanced or "ripened". Other courts have referred to a "maturing business opportunity, which the corporation is actively pursuing". The analysis is so fact-specific that little is gained from broad statements of principle in this area. Directors must be sensitive to the concept of appropriation of corporate opportunities and its implications and should obtain legal advice when they are considering a course of action that could be construed as an appropriation of corporate opportunity. If the corporation declines an opportunity, a director should have definitive and well-documented evidence of this before passing the information about the opportunity on to someone else or taking advantage of it himself or herself. Directors who may wish to pursue an opportunity once the corporation has rejected it (or wish to pass it on to someone else), would be wise not to be involved in a decision by the corporation to decline the opportunity, or seek to influence that decision.

Corporate opportunity – the Canaero decision

The Supreme Court of Canada decision in Canaero is the leading case in the area of corporate opportunity. It dealt with the actions of two senior officers of Canaero, but its findings are equally applicable to corporate directors since both directors and senior officers are subject to the same fiduciary duty in their dealings with the corporation they serve.

Mr. O'Malley and Mr. Zarzycki had been involved in Canaero's efforts to obtain a contract for a topographical survey and mapping of parts of Guyana. In July 1966, the Canadian government agreed in principle to provide a loan to the government of Guyana for a project of this nature and Canaero was placed on the list of companies eligible to be awarded the contract. Several weeks later, Mr. O'Malley and Mr. Zarzycki resigned from Canaero and formed their own company, which ultimately won the contract. The Court found that they had breached their fiduciary duty to Canaero and that they were liable to Canaero for the profits they earned from the contract. It didn't matter that Canaero might not have won the contract (and likely could not have won the contract since it did not satisfy the Canadian ownership requirements which the Canadian government imposed as a requirement for the successful bidder). It was not necessary for Canaero to prove that it would have made a profit from the contract or how much that profit would have been — it was entitled to receive all of the profits that its two former officers had earned.

The general standards of loyalty, good faith and avoidance of a conflict of duty and self-interest to which the conduct of a director or senior officer must conform, must be tested in each case by many factors which it would be reckless to attempt to enumerate exhaustively. Among them are the factor of position or office held, the nature of the corporate opportunity, its ripeness, its specificness and the director's or managerial officer's relation to it, the amount of knowledge possessed, the circumstances in which it was obtained and whether it was special or, indeed, even private, the factor of time in the continuation of fiduciary duty where the alleged breach occurs after termination of the relationship with the company, and the circumstances under which the relationship was terminated, that is whether by retirement or resignation or discharge.

Canadian Aero Service Ltd. v. O'Malley (1973), 11 C.P.R. (2d) 206 (S.C.C.)

Duty of Confidentiality

The directors' fiduciary duty requires that they protect information about the corporation which is confidential or proprietary to the corporation. This restriction prevents directors and officers from using such information to their own advantage at the corporation's expense but may also complicate relationships the directors and officers have with others outside the corporation. For example, it may be difficult for a director who represents an investor not to disclose to his or her employer certain confidential details about the corporation's financial position. Nevertheless, the director may be bound by his or her fiduciary duty not to do so.

Duty to Disclose

In some circumstances, directors may be under an obligation to disclose information to the corporation, which the director has by virtue of another relationship. The courts have not said that directors must share everything they know with the corporation. However, if the information affects the corporation in a "vital aspect of its business", the courts have found there to be a duty to disclose. There are no bright line tests in this area that will tell a director definitively that certain information goes to the corporation's vital interests and must therefore be disclosed to the corporation. Accordingly, it will be advisable in many cases for a director to obtain legal advice. As discussed below, the statutory due diligence defence available for breach of duty of care will allow a director to rely in good faith on an opinion of counsel.

LEADING DECISION

Duty to disclose – the Gemini decision

Two competing airlines — Air Canada and PWA (which then owned Canadian Airlines) — were partners in a computerized reservation system operated by a corporation called Gemini. Air Canada and PWA each nominated two of their employees to serve as directors on the board of Gemini. PWA later began negotiating a strategic alliance with American Airlines. The two PWA nominees to the Gemini board were participating in these negotiations with American Airlines and were bound by a confidentiality agreement not to disclose the negotiations. Part of the strategic alliance would involve Canadian Airlines withdrawing from Gemini's reservation system and joining Sabre, American Airline's reservation system. The two PWA nominees to the Gemini board were participating in the negotiations with American Airlines and were bound by a confidentiality agreement. They did not tell anyone at Gemini about these discussions. The Ontario Court of Appeal found that these two directors had breached their fiduciary duty to Gemini in not disclosing to Gemini information that affected Gemini "in a vital aspect of its business".
PWA Corp. v. Gemini Group Automated Distribution Systems Inc. (1993), 8 B.L.R. (2d) 221 (Ont. Gen. Div. [Commercial List]), additional reasons at (1993), 8 B.L.R. (2d) 221n, affirmed (1993), 10 B.L.R. (2d) 109 (Ont. C.A.), leave to appeal refused (1993), 10 B.L.R. (2d) 244 (note) (S.C.C.)

Irreconcilable Differences

It is clear to most directors that they must not act in their own self-interests at the expense of the corporation they serve. But what happens if a director owes a fiduciary duty to another person that conflicts directly with his or her fiduciary duty to the corporation? What, for example, should a director do if he or she owes a duty both to the corporation to keep certain information confidential and is under a positive obligation to another person (such as an employer) to disclose that information? This type of situation is referred to as an "untenable position" for a director — a no win proposition. The director will necessarily breach the fiduciary duty he or she owes to one organization or the other. The only way to deal with these situations is to avoid them. This involves thinking potential conflicts through carefully before agreeing to sit on a board. Once on the board, if the director recognizes a potential for the duty owed to the corporation to collide with the duty owed to another person, the director should seriously consider resigning from the board. Directors who find themselves caught in the untenable position of owing conflicting fiduciary duties should consult their own legal counsel (i.e., not the corporation's counsel) for advice in navigating out of the situation.

DUTY OF CARE

What Does the Duty of Care Require?

How good a job must a director do? By what standard will his or her performance be judged? The standard of performance required of directors is set out in the corporate statutes and requires every director to *exercise the care, diligence and skill that a reasonably prudent person would exercise in comparable circumstances.* This is referred to as the director's "duty of care".

The duty of care requires directors to spend the time necessary to make an informed business judgment. Directors who are being careful and diligent will ask themselves whether they have the information they need in order to make a decision, will consider that information critically and will question management and outside advisors closely until they are satisfied with the responses they receive. Only then will they apply their business judgment to the matter before them.

How careful and diligent must the director be? The standard is what a "reasonably prudent person" would do "in comparable circumstances". The words "reasonably prudent" mean that directors will not be held to a standard of infallibility or that they must be extraordinarily conservative in their judgments. The standard of a "reasonably prudent person" takes into account the fact that there is risk involved in running a business.

The words "in comparable circumstances" allows a court to consider all aspects of an impugned transaction in determining whether a director has acted in accordance with his or her duty of care. This may include the kind of business carried on by the corporation, the nature of the transaction in question, the relationship of the director to the corporation (for example, whether the director is also a member of management) and the expertise and experience of the director. It may include the time available to the directors to make certain decisions. While directors should strongly resist being rushed into decisions by management or by arbitrary deadlines set by other parties to a transaction, there will be circumstances in which the directors will have a finite amount of time in which to consider an issue. One example is when the corporation is the subject of a hostile bid. Another is when the corporation experiences a catastrophic event, such as an explosion at one of its plants. Where the time constraints are real, they will be among the "circumstances" that a court will take into account in determining whether the directors discharged their duty of care.

Directors are often concerned about the degree of "skill" required of them. Will they be criticized for not recognizing an issue that they do not have the expertise to detect? Courts will deal harshly with directors who turn a blind eye to a problem. However, directors are not required to have any particular set of skills. They are only expected to use the skill they do possess for the benefit of the corporation. Directors must apply whatever knowledge, education and experience they have to the business and affairs of the corporation and when particular skills or expertise is required that the directors do not possess, to seek out the experience and expertise of others. (See "June 2003 Update" for YBM decision on this point.)

Are All Directors Subject to the Same Duty?

Directors are often concerned about whether they will be subject to a different standard if they sit on the audit committee, the environmental committee, a special committee or any other committee of the board. The answer is that all directors are subject to the same duty of care. The variable is the "comparable circumstances" in which they find themselves. As discussed above, a director must exercise the care, diligence and skill that a reasonably prudent person would exercise *in comparable circumstances*. If a director has received information or insight about a particular matter as a result of sitting on a committee, that information or insight becomes part of the "comparable circumstances" against which a court may judge the director's conduct. The criticism of directors who are seen as having failed from a governance perspective has had little to do with their skills, but rather with their failure to deal effectively with the circumstances in which they found themselves. Enron was a leading example.

Directors are also often concerned about whether the particular skills they possess will impose a higher duty of care on them. This issue has attracted a great deal of attention recently because of introduction of requirements by U.S. stock exchanges that all members of the audit committee be "financially literate" and that at least one member of the audit committee be a "financial expert" (referred to as an "audit committee financial expert" under Sarbanes-Oxley). Again, the answer is that all directors are subject to the same duty of care. They are required to apply the skills they have to the exercise of their responsibilities as directors. If they have financial expertise, they must apply it. It is of course true that if a problem arises with the corporation's financial statements, those directors with financial expertise will be front and centre in any litigation. The same will of course be true in other situations - the diligence of a lawyer, scientist or engineer on the board will be particularly closely scrutinized if the corporation faces problems in areas within their expertise. However, the test of whether a director with particular expertise was negligent will be whether he or she exercised the care, diligence and skill that a reasonably prudent person would have exercised in comparable circumstances—the same test that will be applied to all of the other directors.

DUTY TO OTHER STAKEHOLDERS

Directors owe a fiduciary duty to the corporation. This is the cornerstone of a director's relationship with the corporation and is discussed in detail above.

Under Canadian law, directors owe no separate duty to the shareholders, although the interests of the corporation will usually be the same as the interests of the shareholders taken as a whole. Although there is no specific provision to this effect in any legislature, it is generally accepted in the United States and Canada that the corporation's *raison d'être* is to enhance shareholder value. This is not necessarily the case elsewhere in the world, where the interests of other stakeholders are more integral to the duties of directors.

Fiduciary duty – the Canero decision

The Supreme Court of Canada has been very clear about the importance of holding directors to a very strict standard in terms of their fiduciary duty. Then Chief Justice Bora Laskin reviewed a number of decisions dealing with the fiduciary duty in his decision in Canaero and made the following observations:

> *What these decisions indicate is an updating of the equitable principle whose roots lie in the general standards that I have already mentioned, namely, loyalty, good faith and avoidance of a conflict of duty and self-interest. Strict application against directors and senior management officials is simply recognition of the degree of control which their positions give them in corporate operations, a control which rises above day-to-day accountability to owning shareholders and which comes under some scrutiny only at annual general or at special meetings. It is a necessary supplement, in the public interest, of statutory regulation and accountability which themselves are, at one and the same time, an acknowledgment of the importance of the corporation in the life of the community*

and of the need to compel obedience by it and by its
promoters, directors and managers to norms of exem-
plary behaviour.

(Emphasis added.)
Canadian Aero Service Ltd. v. O'Malley (1973), 11 C.P.R. (2d)
206 (S.C.C.)

Duty to the Corporation's Creditors

Directors often ask whether they owe any duty to the corporation's creditors. Typically, but not always, this comes up when the corporation is insolvent and some of the corporation's creditors have not been paid. They may then sue the directors in an effort to recover some of the amounts owed to them.

The law in Canada on this question is unsettled. Courts in other jurisdictions, including the United States and Australia, have dealt with this issue extensively and have found that, in some cases, the directors owe a fiduciary duty to the creditors. While the courts in Canada have considered applying the same reasoning, they have clearly had some difficulty in doing so. This may be in large part because of the differences between the law in Canada and the law in other jurisdictions. The Quebec Court of Appeal recently reversed a lower court decision that seemed to find that the director of Peoples Department Stores owed a duty to the corporation's creditor's. The former director's of Dylex Corporation are currently being sued on the basis that they owed a duty to the creditors of Dylex. Because the law in this area is far from clear at this point, directors can anticipate that courts will continue to be prepared to consider an argument made by creditors that the directors should be held personally liable in some circumstances when they have not been repaid.

Other Stakeholders

Directors are often concerned with the extent to which they are entitled (or required) to take the interests of stakeholders other than shareholders into account. There can be tension between the desire of many directors to balance the interests of a variety of stakeholders, the view that enhancing shareholder value is the only legitimate purpose of a for-profit organization and the legal obligation of the board to act with a view to the best interests of the corporation.

A corporation's stakeholders include (in addition to its shareholders) its employees, suppliers, customers, creditors, competitors and the community in which it operates. None of the Canadian corporate statutes specifically provides that the directors may take the interests of other stakeholders into account (with the exception of the corporate statutes that allow creditors or employees to elect directors), but it is generally accepted that they may do so, provided that they are acting at all times "honestly and in good faith with a view to the best interests of the corporation". Many of the U.S. corporate statutes have what is referred to as a "constituency provision", which provides that directors are entitled to, but have no duty to, take the interest of the stakeholders into account. Although none of the Canadian statutes specifically prohibits directors from taking the interests of other stakeholders into account, they also do not specifically permit them to do so.

Nominee Directors

It is common for persons who have a significant interest in the corporation to nominate certain individuals to act as directors of the corporation. In a private corporation controlled by one person, that person will typically nominate the entire board. Other stakeholders (such as minority shareholders and other investors) may also acquire a right (generally under a contract such as a shareholders agreement) to nominate individuals to act as directors (see Part II).

The courts have been very clear that the fact of a director having been nominated to the board by a particular person does not entitle that director to prefer the interests of that person to the interests of the corporation. A director must be concerned first and foremost with the interest of the corporation. As an Ontario court put it, the corporate life of a nominee director who votes against the interests of his or her nominator "may be neither happy nor long", but that director must nevertheless act in the best interests of the corporation.

Nominee directors – the Ballard decision

One of the decisions relating to the battle for control of Maple Leaf Gardens in Toronto dealt extensively with whether directors nominated to a board of directors by Harold Ballard had breached their duty to the corporation by simply acting in accordance with Mr. Ballard's wishes.

Mr. Ballard had formed HEB Ltd. in the 1960s as a holding company for his interest in Maple Leaf Gardens Limited and for the benefit of his three children. By the 1980s, the children held the common shares of HEB Ltd., but Mr. Ballard retained control (including the ability to select the board) through the preferred shares he held. Mr. Ballard ultimately decided that he wished to reacquire the common shares from his children, which he accomplished with the support of his friends on the board through a series of corporate transactions that left him holding 68% of the common shares of HEB Ltd. Mr. Justice Farley criticized the directors who were serving on the board of HEB Ltd. at Mr. Ballard's request, and who had exercised their powers as directors to support Mr. Ballard's wishes without question:

> It may well be that the corporate life of a nominee director who votes against the interest of his "appointing" shareholder will be neither happy nor long. However, the role that any director must play (whether or not a nominee director) is that he must act in the best interests of the corporation....The nominee director's obligation to his "appointing" shareholder would seem to me to include the duty to tell the appointer that his requested course of action is wrong if the director in fact feels this way. Such advice, although likely initially unwelcome, may well be valuable to the appointer in the long run. The nominee director cannot be a "Yes man"; he must be an analytical person who can say "Yes" or "No" as the occasion requires (or to put it another way, as the corporation requires).

820099 Ontario Inc. v. Harold E. Ballard Ltd. (1991), 3 B.L.R. (2d) 113 (Ont. Div. Ct.)

Nominee directors – Deluce Holdings v. Air Canada

The nominee directors of Air Canada on the board of Air Ontario Inc. were subject to similar criticism when they terminated William Deluce's employment with Air Ontario. Air Canada held 75% of the shares of Air Ontario and was entitled to nominate seven of the board's ten directors. Deluce Holdings held 25% of the shares and was entitled to nominate the remaining three directors.

The agreement when Air Canada acquired its interest in Air Ontario was that William Deluce (the sole shareholder of Air Ontario) would be responsible for the day-to-day operation of the business but that when Mr. Deluce's employment relationship with Air Ontario terminated, Air Canada would have the option to acquire Deluce Holdings' shares in Air Ontario.

In the spring of 1991, Air Canada changed its policy on its relationship with regional carriers in which it held an equity interest, such as Air Ontario, deciding to acquire a 100% interest in these carriers and operate them directly. The Air Ontario board terminated Mr. Deluce's employment and Air Canada moved to exercise its option to acquire the remaining shares of Air Ontario. Deluce Holdings succeeded in its oppression action against Air Canada. Mr. Justice Blair offered the following comments on the conduct of Air Canada's nominees to the Air Ontario board:

> Under s. 122 of the CBCA directors have a duty, amongst other things, (a) to act honestly and in good faith with a view to the best interests of the corporation, and (b) to comply with any unanimous shareholder agreement. In considering whether or not the directors have complied with these obligations in a given situation more is required than a mere assertion of good faith on the part of the directors. There will almost always be a tension between the directors' position as a director of the corporation in question and the director's position as a shareholder or the nominee of a shareholder. Where an issue arises, hindsight and after-the-fact rationalizations all too

naturally make it easy for the directors to believe that they were, indeed, acting for the benefit of the corporation.

(Emphasis added.)

And further:

> As I have indicated, the evidence here strongly supports a conclusion that, in causing the Air Ontario board to terminate the employment of Mr. Deluce, the Air Canada nominees were acting to carry out an Air Canada agenda and made little, if any, analysis of what was in the best interests of Air Ontario. Whether, had they done so, such an analysis might have yielded sufficient reasons from Air Ontario's perspective to carry out the act of termination, is not the point. Not only was there no "reasonable analysis of the situation" form [sic] that perspective, the question which was uppermost in the minds of the directors was to effect Air Canada's *newly developed corporate objective, it would appear.*

(Emphasis added.)

Deluce Holdings Inc. v. Air Canada (1992), 12 O.R. (3d) 131 (Ont. Gen. Div. [Commercial List])

THE BUSINESS JUDGMENT RULE

The courts in Canada will generally not substitute their own business judgment for that of the directors of a corporation if the directors acted in a manner consistent with their fiduciary duty and duty of care in reaching their decision. This "business judgment rule" shields the decisions of directors from judicial second-guessing if those business decisions were made honestly, prudently, in good faith and on reasonable grounds. As one court said, "... in such cases, the board's decisions will not be subject to microscopic examination and the court will be reluctant to interfere and usurp the board of directors' function in managing the corporation."

It will, of course, be important that the steps taken to reach an informed decision be documented so that, should the decision of the board come under scrutiny at a later date, the board will be able to demonstrate that it had an appropriate process.

Compensation committees – Repap decision

In the Repap decision, the Court used its authority under the oppression remedy to set aside a compensation arrangement with Steven Berg, the former chair of the corporation. It refused to defer to the business judgment of Repap directors in approving these arrangements because, in its view, the directors had not exercised any business judgment.

Repap had been struggling for some time. In 1997, over-leverage and depressed paper prices forced it to dispose of most of its assets (leaving it with only a coated paper plant in New Brunswick) and to convert a significant amount of its debt into equity. Paloma Partners became its largest shareholder as a result of this debt conversion. In 1998, Repap completed a debt restructuring, which left it cash poor. It closed its head office in Montreal, reduced head office staff from 80 to five — four of whom moved to Stamford, Connecticut, where the sales staff was located.

In late 1998, Mr. Berg developed an interest in Repap. By January 1999 he had arranged for Third Avenue Funds to acquire the Paloma Partners interest in Repap, invested some of his own funds and become a director and chair of Repap. In March 1999, Repap entered into an employment arrangement with Mr. Berg under which he became Chairman and Senior Executive Officer of Repap. Those arrangements included a five-year employment term with renewals, a signing bonus of 25 million shares, a stock option grant of 75 million shares, a market capitalization bonus, immediate pension credit of eight years, executive employee benefits and generous change of control and termination provisions.

The decision refers to various evidence that Repap did not need Mr. Berg's services and that there was no executive role for him. It is clear from the facts laid out in this decision that Mr. Berg used his position on the board to drive this arrangement through.

The board turned down the proposed arrangements with Mr. Berg when they were presented to them in February 1999 and one director resigned to signal his objections. A short time later, one of the Third Avenue nominees, who had been chair of the compensation committee, also resigned. Mr. Berg recruited two new directors, one of whom became chair of the compensation committee. In March, the board approved the compensation arrangements. Two of the three members of the compensation committee met for less than 10 minutes prior to that meeting. The board itself devoted only about 30 minutes to the matter. It received a report from outside counsel (whose independence from Mr. Berg was highly questionable) which included a report from a compensation expert. The Court noted that although the compensation expert was highly qualified, she was not given all of the relevant facts or the time necessary to do the appropriate analysis. As a result, her opinion was highly qualified. None of the members of the board asked any questions about her expert report.

The Court set the contract aside and in the course of its decision found that the board had not discharged its duty of care in approving the arrangements with Mr. Berg. It noted as follows:

> The business judgment rule protects Boards and directors from those that might second-guess their decisions. The court looks to see that the directors made a reasonable decision, not a perfect decision. This approach recognizes the autonomy and integrity of a corporation and the expertise of its directors. They are in the advantageous position of investigating and considering first-hand the circumstances that come before it and are in a far better position than a court to understand the affairs of the corporation and to guide its operation.

UPM-Kymmene Corp. v. UPM-Kymmene Miramichi Inc., [2002] O.J. No. 2412 (Ont. S.C.J. [Commercial List])

There is a similar, but not identical business judgment rule for directors under U.S. law. In the United States, there is a presumption that directors' decisions have been made on an informed basis, in good faith and with the honest belief that the action taken was in the best interests of the company. To overcome this presumption, a plaintiff must show not only that the director failed to exercise his or her duty of care, but that the director was "grossly negligent" in failing to do so. In other words, the onus is on the plaintiff to rebut the presumption that the directors acted properly. This is different from the approach taken by Canadian courts, which do not assume that the directors behaved appropriately, but instead review the processes followed by the directors in reaching their decision to determine whether those processes were in fact appropriate.

DUE DILIGENCE

What Is Due Diligence?

"Due diligence" in the context of directors' duties generally refers to the review and investigation the directors conduct before reaching a decision with respect to any particular matter. Failure on the part of a director to be duly diligent can result in personal liability for that director. However, if the director has reviewed and investigated the matter appropriately, then the director will have a "due diligence defence" against any action taken against him or her with respect to that matter. (See "June 2003 Update" for YBM decision on this point.)

Some statutes are quite specific about what the directors may rely on in order to be able to establish a due diligence defence. For example, under most of the corporate statutes, if the director relied in good faith on certain financial statements or reports of certain professional advisors, that director has a defence against personal liability imposed in connection with specific actions of the corporation. Other statutes do not prescribe any particular action which will shield a director from liability. Under securities laws, for example, if the directors had "reasonable grounds" for believing that there was no misrepresentation in a prospectus, they will have a due diligence defence if any purchaser of the securities in question seeks to sue them. The one significant area for which there is no due diligence defence is liability for employee wages (Part VI).

Of course, if a director is sued, it is not enough that the director exercised due diligence—he or she will also have to be able to prove it. Documenting the diligence conducted by the directors is therefore critical. Generally, it is wise to have this done through the corporate secretary or legal counsel, so that careful consideration can be given to what should be preserved as part of the permanent record, although the directors should be comfortable with how this record is being developed and maintained. Whether directors should keep their own notes is an issue for discussion. While in some cases, a director may be happy to have some evidence in his or her own file of having raised a particular issue, in many other cases, the notes the director has made in the margin of the board agenda or the comments the director has written on the presentation materials may provide evidence of questions or concerns which were not raised or thoroughly pursued. A director should discuss these issues with legal counsel and develop a consistent methodology for dealing with notes and drafts. See Part III.

Reliance

Directors do not typically assemble the information they need to discharge their responsibilities themselves — they rely on management (and on outside advisors) to provide them with that information (see Part I). Nor do they typically analyze that information themselves; when they receive the information, it has been processed and filtered by management and by outside advisors. The discussion below describes the elements of a sustainable due diligence when directors are relying on information and analysis provided by others.

The Good Faith Requirement

An integral part of any due diligence defence is that the directors must have relied on the information, analysis, advice and opinions they received "in good faith". "Good faith" reliance means that the directors have not blindly accepted what they have heard — they have asked themselves whether it seems reasonable and have tested the basis of the facts and analysis. It also means that the directors know of no reason to doubt the honesty or integrity of the person dealing with the board and no reason to think that the person may be acting out of self-interest in providing that information.

Reliance on Management

It is well accepted that the board does not manage the business and affairs of the corporation itself, but that it may delegate to management responsibility for the day-to-day operations of the corporation's business. The corollary of this is that the board must rely on management to provide it with information about the corporation's operations and other factors necessary to allow the board to discharge its oversight function.

Directors are often concerned about whether they will be blamed if management deliberately misleads or provides them with incomplete or incorrect information. In the absence of grounds for suspicion, and the board has exercised "due diligence" where appropriate, the board is entitled to rely on the honesty and integrity of management.

Reliance on Financial Statements

Some statutory due diligence defences protect directors from liability if they relied *in good faith* on certain financial statements. It is important to note that the financial statements must be accompanied by some comfort that those statements present fairly the financial position of the corporation in accordance with GAAP (note, however, that the CBCA does not refer to GAAP). This comfort must be provided in the form of:

- a representation from an officer of the corporation (which need not be in writing); or
- a written report of the corporation's auditor.

Reliance on Outside Advisors

Directors are also entitled to rely in good faith on reports of certain persons (such as lawyers, accountants, engineers and appraisers) whose profession (or expertise) lends credibility to a statement made by that person. The board will often need to rely on professional advisors in reaching a decision. The fact that the directors have relied on advisors with professional accreditation will not, however, be sufficient. Two elements must be present for the directors to have relied on the advice of such professionals *in good faith*. First, they must be appropriately qualified advisors. The courts have, for example, referred with approval to directors relying on "competent professional technical staff", "competent legal advice" and "consultants of national reputation". Second, the advisors must have the information and context necessary to allow the advisors to give appropriate advice. Failing to disclose all of the details of a transaction to outside counsel can, for example, lead to the directors not being able to use that counsel's opinion as a defence.

Reliance on outside advisors – Westfair

In the Westfair decision, the board of directors had obtained legal advice from two major law firms in connection with its decision to pay a dividend of 100% of the previous year's retained earnings. Both firms provided opinions that the payment of dividends out of retained earnings would not be held to be oppressive, unfairly prejudicial to, or unfairly disregard the interests of the Class A shareholders. The Court found, however, that there were additional facts relevant to the impact of this dividend on the Class A shareholders (that the company planned to borrow the amount of the dividend back from the common shareholders). Because the two law firms did not have the benefit of all of the facts, the Court held that the board could not rely on those opinions as part of its due diligence defence.

Westfair Foods Ltd. v. Watt, [1990] 4 W.W.R. 685 (Alta. Q.B.), affirmed [1991] 4 W.W.R. 695 (Alta. C.A.), leave to appeal refused (1991), [1992] 1 W.W.R. lxv (S.C.C.)

PART V

When It's Not Business as Usual

WHAT DOES "OUTSIDE OF THE ORDINARY COURSE OF BUSINESS" MEAN?

A transaction or issue that is within the "ordinary course of a corporation's business" is one that relates to the day-to-day operation of the corporation's business. For example, if a corporation is in the business of manufacturing appliances, then hiring employees to work in the factory, ordering parts from suppliers and selling the appliances to its customers would all be considered to be within the ordinary course of the corporation's business. However, building a new factory would be outside the ordinary course of business, since the corporation is in the business of manufacturing appliances and not in the business of building factories.

The significance of an issue or transaction being outside of the ordinary course of business from a governance perspective is that, generally speaking, it requires board approval. The authority delegated to management by the board is usually restricted to matters that are within the ordinary course of the corporation's business. If management proposes to take any material action which goes beyond this delegated authority, it must return to the board for authority to proceed. The board reviews management's analysis and proposals and either approves or rejects management's recommended course of action or returns the matter to management for further consideration. If the corporation is faced with a crisis of some type, the board's oversight responsibilities may also require it to become involved in the corporation's handling of the crisis until it is satisfied that the matter is under control and being appropriately handled by management.

What directors should do when faced with matters that are outside the corporation's ordinary course of business is no different than what they should do in the discharge of their responsibilities on a day-to-day basis. They must perform their oversight function in a manner that is consistent with their fiduciary duty and duty of care. How exactly they should go about doing this depends very much on the particular circumstances. A brief discussion of some of the considerations directors should keep in mind when they are dealing with major transactions, with financial instability and with corporate crises is set out below.

MAJOR TRANSACTIONS

Major transactions include acquisitions, dispositions, financings, joint ventures, reorganizations and mergers, to name just a few. It is important that the board be engaged in the evaluation of the transaction as early on as possible so that they have the time necessary to reach an informed business judgment without unduly delaying the transaction (and potentially compromising the interests of the corporation). The need to keep the board in the loop must, of course, be balanced with not overloading the board with information about potential opportunities which management has not yet had the time to evaluate fully.

When a major transaction is brought to the board, the directors should make certain that:

- they have the information they need — generally this information will be provided by management, but there may be situations in which the board wishes to reach out to advisors and consultants for additional information
- they are getting the right advice — the appropriate advisors and consultants should be engaged and be provided with the information necessary for them to give relevant advice to the board
- they are taking the time they need to reach an informed decision — transactions can be inherently time sensitive, putting additional pressure on the directors who often have other full-time commitments

- the process is independent — involvement by directors who have a relationship with anyone with an interest in a transaction could taint the independence of the process, thereby exposing the corporation and possibly the directors to action by those who feel they have been harmed by the actions of the corporation and its board.
- they have considered the interests of any stakeholder (such as minority shareholders or creditors) who would be adversely affected by the course of action being contemplated by the board of directors — directors may find their decisions subsequently challenged by certain of these stakeholders under the oppression remedy (see Part VI).

Transactions that involve a change of control of the corporation (for example, pursuant to a take-over bid) give rise to particular issues for directors. Canadian courts have held, for example, that the board's duty in these circumstances is to maximize shareholder value (except where there is a controlling shareholder, in which case the directors will have little impact on the process). It is important that the board receive the appropriate legal advice in a timely fashion to be sure that it is discharging its responsibilities in specialized circumstances as the law requires.

LEADING DECISION

Role of the board in a merger – Smith v. Van Gorkom

Trans Union was a large American public company. In the early 1980s its chairman, Jerome Van Gorkom, agreed to a merger of Trans Union with a company in the Marmon Group of companies. The deal paid shareholders $55 a share at a time when the shares were trading at $38. The shareholders approved the transaction.

In spite of all of this, the Court found that the directors had breached their duty of care (which is similar to the duty of care in Canada). The problem was not the result, but the process the directors had followed in approving the transaction. Although Mr. Van Gorkom had put the deal in front of them with no advance warning, and they were given no information to review in advance of the meeting, the directors approved the transaction after only two hours. The fact that the shareholders received a significant premium for their shares was irrelevant, because the directors did not know what Trans Union's value was and were therefore not in a position to assess the adequacy of the premium.

The Court found that the directors were grossly negligent in approving the sale of Trans Union upon two hours' consideration, without prior notice and without the exigency of a crisis or emergency. It was not enough that there was no fraud or bad faith on the part of the Trans Union board. The Court stated that directors have a duty to inform themselves prior to making a business decision of all material information reasonably available to them, and to assess such information with a critical eye.

Smith v. Van Gorkom, 488 A.2d 858 (Del. Supr. 1985)

The role of board in related party transactions – the KeepRite decision

The KeepRite decision involved a transaction in which KeepRite acquired assets from two of its affiliates (wholly-owned subsidiaries of KeepRite's majority shareholder). The KeepRite board established an independent committee that met five times over a six-week period and evaluated information about the transaction provided to it from a variety of sources. The Court found that the independent committee carried out its function in an appropriate and independent manner — it was aware of its mandate, was at all times conscious that this was not an arm's-length transaction and assessed the benefits of the transaction to KeepRite.

Brant Investments Ltd. v. KeepRite Inc. (1991), 3 O.R. (3d) 289 (Ont. C.A.)

The business judgment rule in the context of a take-over bid – the Schneider decision

The Schneider decision dealt with an unsolicited take-over bid by Maple Leaf Foods Inc. for the shares of Schneider Corporation. The Court observed that the duty of directors of a company that is the target of a take-over bid is a rapidly developing area of law, but provided the following comfort for directors who follow an appropriate process:

> If a board of directors has acted on the advice of a committee composed of persons having no conflict of interest, and that committee has acted independently, in good faith, and made an informed recommendation as to the best available transaction for the shareholders in the circumstances, the business judgment rule applies.

Pente Investment Management Ltd. v. Schneider Corp. (1998), 113 O.A.C. 253 (Ont. C.A.)

DEALING WITH A CRISIS

When a corporation faces a crisis—whether it is fraud within the organization, significant litigation, liabilities or losses, or a restatement of the corporation's financial statements—the corporation will need the leadership and experience of its board. There are three stages for any crisis—before the crisis occurs, while the crisis is ongoing and after the crisis has passed. There is a role for the board at each stage.

Before a Crisis Occurs

Since crises by definition arise with little or no warning, the best that most organizations can do from a planning perspective is to develop a generic response plan which could be adapted and implemented if the need arose. The role of the board at this stage is to review the plan developed by management. The following are among the issues that might be considered in this type of plan:

- Who in the organization should be contacted immediately if a crisis should occur (this typically includes some combination of the CEO, CFO, general counsel, corporate secretary and investor relations specialist) and when will other key players (including the rest of the board) be advised.
- Who from outside the organization should be consulted if a crisis should occur (this list typically includes outside counsel, the auditor and a public relations specialist).
- Who in the organization will be responsible for dealing with this crisis (the full board? a committee of the board? the CEO? some other member of management?).
- Who will speak for the organization.
- Are there any regulators or enforcement bodies that need to be advised.
- What are the corporation's public disclosure obligations.
- What steps need to be taken in order to preserve relevant evidence.
- What immediate action, if any, should be taken with respect to suspected wrongdoers.
- Which professional advisors should be engaged.
- Where should information with respect to this matter be kept and meetings with respect to this matter be held.
- How should information be communicated to shareholders.

BEST PRACTICE

Investor relations

The investor relations function has assumed increased importance in recent years, as issuers have dealt with the crisis in investor confidence and increased regulatory focus on disclosure issues. Investor relations professionals play an important role in the ordinary course of an issuer's activities, but will be critical to the implementation of an effective strategy as a corporation navigates through a crisis or deals with a major transaction.

In Canada, the investor relations profession is represented by Canadian Investor Relations Institute

("CIRI") . CIRI describes the investor relations function as follows:

> Investor relations is a corporate activity combining the disciplines of finance, marketing and communications, which provides present and potential investors with an accurate portrayal of a company's performance and prospects so that they can make properly informed investment decisions. Effective investor relations should have a positive effect on the market's assessment of a company's value relative to that of the overall market, thereby minimizing the company's cost of capital, and should serve as a conduit for providing market intelligence to corporate management.

CIRI's website is www.ciri.org.

When a Crisis Has Occurred

The actual course of action that the corporation should follow if a crisis occurs will depend on the nature and specifics of the crisis. One of the issues to be addressed early on is how the directors will discharge their responsibilities effectively. Although no director should feel excluded from the process (unless there is a conflict which makes such exclusion necessary), the most efficient way to deal with a crisis is often to strike a committee of the board to deal with the matter. This is the case particularly where there is a large board. Because meetings will be frequent and often long, it may be impractical to call full meetings of the board as necessary. Where a special committee is struck to deal with the crisis, it will be important to include in the mandate of that committee a requirement that it report regularly to the full board.

The second important consideration in determining how the board will deal with the crisis is, of course, the independence issue. If the crisis involves some alleged impropriety on the part of the CEO, it goes without saying that the CEO should be excluded from board or committee deliberations, except to the extent that particular information from that individual is required. Similarly, there may be situations in which the inclusion of directors with a relationship with a major shareholder would compromise the independence of the process, or create the perception on the part of others that the process was not independent.

A regular flow of information to the board or special committee will be critical to the ability of the directors to satisfy their obligations. The board or special committee should also be satisfied that it is receiving appropriate advice from outside advisors.

After the Crisis Has Passed

After the crisis has passed, the board should oversee a process that has two objectives. First, it should evaluate how the corporation responded to the crisis — what it did well and what it would have liked to have done better. Its procedures for dealing with these situations should be revised accordingly. Everyone who played a role in navigating through the crisis — both inside and outside of the organization — should be invited to provide input into this process.

Second, the review process should seek to determine how the crisis arose in the first place and what steps need to be taken in order to avoid a similar occurrence. Is there a problem with internal controls? Are there issues that need to be addressed through employee education? Does the corporation have the right management and is management setting an ethical tone for the corporation that will support corrective action?

FINANCIAL INSTABILITY

Guiding a company through a financial crisis is one of the most difficult challenges a board director can face. The directors may not have seen the crisis coming. They may feel responsible for not having been able to help the corporation to avoid the crisis or that management has not been candid with them, leaving them with a critical situation which they may feel could have been avoided. Many directors will be dealing with issues of solvency for the first time and may be uncertain about how to evaluate the options presented to them by management.

It may be difficult to anticipate sudden changes in the corporation's external environment that may compromise the corporation's financial position. However, directors — even those without formal training in accounting — should learn to recognize certain warning signs. For example, the company's inability to meet its budget may be an early sign of problems, particularly if management is not able to explain discrepancies from the budget to the directors' satisfaction.

Directors should also be wary of unexplained or unexpected changes in plans. For example, a sudden decision by management to abandon a financing proposal may in fact reflect an inability to complete the financing on the terms approved by the board. The lenders may have developed a different view of the corporation's financial condition than what the board understands it to be. The board needs to understand the lender's reservations about the corporation's credit worthiness, together with the implications of these reservations for the corporation to be able to obtain financing in the future.

Directors should also become familiar with the important indicators for the corporation and the industry in which it operates. This information should be readily obtainable from the corporation's CFO and from its auditors.

As in any other situation, the board must be satisfied that it is receiving the information and advice it needs, that its process is thorough and thoughtful and that it is free of any conflict of interest. Directors should be particularly sensitive to the interests of the corporation's creditors as the corporation moves towards insolvency. The current unsettled state of the law in Canada with respect to duties of directors to creditors is described in Part IV.

LEADING DECISION

Duty of care – the Standard Trust decision

At one time, Standard Trust was a large Canadian trust company. It was owned by a public company called Standard Trustco. Following a regulatory investigation in the early 1990s, Standard Trustco and Standard Trust were forced to restate their financial statements, showing a significant loss in place of the profits previously reported. They eventually went into bankruptcy.

The description of the demise of Standard Trust in the OSC decision relating to that issuer provides some interesting examples of a board failing to recognize the signs warning of the company's deteriorating financial condition.

In December 1989, the management presented a projection for the 1989 year-end financial statement to the board of Standard Trustco (Standard Trust's parent company), including the provision for loan losses which management was proposing for the 1989 financial statements. In January 1990, the board approved Standard Trustco's audited financial statements which showed a provision for losses of more than twice what management had presented to the board. The board does not appear to have reacted to this sudden upward change in the loan loss provisions.

In April 1990, the boards of both Standard Trust and Standard Trustco approved the unaudited first quarter financial statements for these companies. The statements for both companies showed loan loss provisions of $2,535,000. This was $2,217,000 higher than what was budgeted for the quarter and almost twice the provision for all of the previous fiscal year. Again, there seems to have been no reaction from either board to this sudden and significant increase in loan loss provisions.

At the conclusion of its action against the two companies and their directors, the Ontario Securities Commission stated that the directors had failed to discharge their duty of care, that is, they had not exercised the care, duty and skill that a reasonably prudent person would exercise in comparable circumstances. The OSC pointed to the financial information provided to the board, showing a deteriorating financial condition which was not ultimately reflected in the financial statements. It also pointed to the fact that the financial institution regulators raised serious concerns about the financial reporting of the two companies and about their financial condition. The OSC listed the actions which the boards should have taken, which included:

- making inquiries of the representatives of the regulators present at the board meetings
- asking the audit committee what inquiries it made and discussions it had made
- asking senior officers about problems in the mortgage portfolio

- asking the auditor about the appropriateness of the accrual policy and reserves, as well as about accounting practices of other financial institutions
- consulting with another accounting firm, particularly in light of the fact that the regulators had raised serious questions about a long-standing accounting policy that had been followed by the company and accepted by the auditor
- providing outside counsel with complete background information and asking for advice relating to the materiality of the regulator's concerns and the course of action it should take from a legal perspective
- asking in-house counsel for advice on disclosure issues
- seeking advice from independent property appraisers.

Re Standard Trustco Ltd (1992), 15 O.S.C.B. 4322, 6 B.L.R. (2d) 241 (O.S.C.)

LIABILITY ISSUES

Directors should always inquire about liability issues when they are dealing with matters outside of the ordinary course of business. Depending on the circumstances of a particular transaction or crisis, directors may be exposed to personal liability in areas which do not arise in the context of the corporation's day-to-day business. Directors should be sure that they know how to discharge their duties to the corporation with respect to matters that go beyond their routine oversight function so that they will have a sustainable due diligence defence if they are sued.

In addition, directors should review their indemnities and their D&O insurance to determine whether there might be any gaps in coverage resulting in the nature of the transaction in which the corporation proposes to engage. For example, if the corporation is struggling with financial instability, directors should be concerned about whether the corporation will be in a position to honour any indemnity it has provided to the directors. In some circumstances it may be possible to obtain an indemnity from another person, such as a controlling shareholder. For most directors, if they run a real risk of personal liability with little prospect of indemnification, it is reasonable to give serious consideration to resigning from the board. Similarly, there may be transactions that give rise to liabilities that D&O insurance will not cover. Very often, for example, a D&O policy will not cover litigation commenced against a board by a major shareholder. Liability issues are discussed in more detail in Part VI.

PART VI

Liability Issues

OVERVIEW OF LIABILITY ISSUES

Serving as a director brings with it exposure to personal liability. Directors have good reason to be concerned about this exposure. The costs of mounting a defence, let alone the amount of any damages or fines the director may be required to pay, can be significant — even financially crippling for some directors.

Although personal liability is, and should be, a concern for directors, two common misperceptions need to be corrected. First, directors are often concerned that if the corporation does anything wrong — breaches its bank covenants, fires an employee or recalls defective products — that the directors can be held liable. That is not the case. Directors are not automatically liable for the actions of the corporation. Although this part of the book describes the various ways in which directors can be held personally liable for certain actions of the corporation, it is important to recognize that the law does not generally view directors as being guarantors of the corporation's conduct. Second, in an environment in which boards and senior management are being held increasingly accountable, there is sometimes a concern that exposure to liability is an unmanageable risk. It is important for directors to understand that the appropriate discharge of their responsibilities will provide them with a defence to virtually any action taken against them (with the important exception of liability for employee wages). The ability of a director to mount a successful defence, of course, depends very much on the director having understood his or her responsibilities and having discharged them effectively in the first place. However, directors should recognise that even where their conduct has been exemplary they can still be sued and the time, energy and money to prove their case can be significant. How a director can manage the risks involved in being sued (whether because of an actual breach of some duty by the director or for tactical reasons) is discussed below.

There is no generic list of potential liabilities which are relevant to all directors of all corporations. The particular liabilities applicable to the members of any given board will depend on a number of factors, including:

- the corporation's jurisdiction of incorporation;
- the geographic regions in which it operates;
- the nature of its business;
- whether it is a public or private corporation; and
- the jurisdictions in which it has security holders.

Directors should obtain specific advice about the types of liability to which they are exposed and how to protect themselves through the exercise of appropriate diligence. They should request this advice when they first join the board. It should be updated for the entire board annually and whenever there are significant legislative or judicial developments relevant to the corporation and its board. It should also be revisited when the board takes certain action, such as declaring dividends or the corporation faces particular challenges, such as a take-over bid or financial instability.

Rather than attempting to catalogue all of the possible areas of liability, this part of the book collects those liabilities in three broad categories: statutory liability for the actions of the corporation, liability under the oppression remedy and liability for a director's own actions.

STATUTORY LIABILITY FOR ACTIONS OF THE CORPORATION

The Rationale for Imposing Personal Liability on Directors

There are literally hundreds of statutes which impose personal liability on directors (and officers). The public policy objective is clear. The individuals who form the corporation's board of directors and management team control the corporation's conduct. Legislators give those individuals a stake in promoting corporate compliance by imposing a cost on them personally for non-compliance.

It is important to note that there are defences available for virtually all statutory liabilities imposed on directors. The one important exception is director liability for unpaid employee wages (discussed in more detail below). In almost all other cases, directors will not be held personally liable for the corporation's breach of a statute unless they authorized the corporation to breach a statute or they failed to discharge their duties as that statute requires in preventing that breach.

Authorizing the Corporation to Commit an Offence
Breach of a statute is typically punishable by a fine, imprisonment or both. For a number of reasons, these penalties may not be effective in deterring a corporation from breaching the statute. First, corporations cannot be sent to prison. Second, the amount of the fine may be inconsequential to the corporation—if the cost of compliance is more than the amount of the fine, the fine is simply a cost of doing business. Third, the individuals responsible for making the corporate decisions may not be concerned about the damage to the corporation's reputation that may result from charges under a statute. Fourth, the individuals behind the corporation may simply be using the corporation as a liability shield—causing it to commit offences for their benefit. Finally, even if the directors are not actively causing the corporation to take action that breaches a statute, they may sit by and allow the corporation to commit that breach, simply because there are no ramifications for them personally if the corporation does so.

Accordingly, in order to encourage compliance by corporations, many statutes provide that, if a corporation commits an offence, the directors (and officers) who "directed", "authorized", "assented to", "participated in", "permitted", "acquiesced" or "concurred" in the offence may themselves be guilty of an offence. The specific wording will depend on the statute, but the purpose of this type of provision is to provide a basis on which to punish the individuals who were responsible for causing the corporation to commit the offence. Directors who were not aware of (but were not wilfully blind to) the corporation's actions or who tried to prevent the corporation from committing the offence will have a defence to action taken against them under these provisions.

This type of personal liability, which is sometimes called "attribution liability", is included in a great many statutes — too many to list here. It generally involves a fine, imprisonment or both. Although the likelihood that a court would imprison a director for the corporation's failure to comply with certain statutory provisions may be remote (particularly where the requirements are administrative in nature, such as filing a particular form), the possibility certainly exists. Fining directors for certain statutory breaches is not at all uncommon.

Liability for Failing to Exercise Due Diligence

Overview
Many statutes use director liability as a way of focusing the attention of the board on particularly important issues. They do this by imposing potentially significant liability on individual directors if the directors failed to exercise "due diligence" in trying to ensure that the corporation complies with these provisions. Each such provision and its accompanying defence will have their own peculiarities that need to be considered in detail in order to understand them thoroughly. To illustrate the approach and range of issues that may arise in these circumstances, see the example of director liability for dividends discussed below.

One Example — Personal Liability for Dividend Payments
Personal liability accompanied by a due diligence defence arises, under the corporate statutes, if the corporation makes certain payments (such as dividends) to its shareholders when it is insolvent (or if the payment would make it insolvent). Directors who approve these payments contrary to the statutes can be made to personally pay back to the corporation the full amount paid contrary to the statute.

The solvency test for the payment of dividends:

A corporation shall not declare or pay a dividend if there are reasonable grounds for believing that

(a) the corporation is, or would after the payment be, unable to pay its liabilities as they become due; or

(b) the realizable value of the corporation's assets would thereby be less than the aggregate of its liabilities and stated capital of all classes.

This test provides some protection to the corporation's creditors — particularly its unsecured trade creditors — by prohibiting the payment of dividends out to the shareholders if the corporation will not be able to pay its creditors. This reflects the basic principle that creditors rank ahead of shareholders. The importance attached to the protection of the corporation's creditors explains why the corporate statutes impose personal liability on individual directors who are responsible for paying corporate funds to shareholders when the corporation is not in a position to honour its obligations to its creditors.

The corporate statutes do not allow any director to be uninvolved in the payment of a dividend. The following provisions operate to impose accountability on every director who was aware of the dividend:

- Only the full board has the authority to approve a dividend — it may not delegate this authority to management or to a committee of the board.
- Any director who "voted for or consented to" the resolution authorizing the dividend contrary to the statute is liable.
- Any director who was at the meeting is deemed to have consented to the resolution unless he or she provides a formal dissent as required by the statute.
- Any director who was not at the meeting is deemed to have consented to the resolution unless he or she provides a formal dissent as required by the statute within seven days after becoming aware of the resolution.

In order to conclude that the dividend is proper and meets the applicable statutory requirements, the board will need to review certain documentation and take advice from certain advisors. The corporate statutes relieve directors of liability if they relied "in good faith" on the following:

- the corporation's financial statements provided that they have the appropriate confirmation from either an officer of the corporation or the external auditor that the statements "present fairly the financial position of the corporation in accordance with generally accepted accounting principles"; or
- the report of a lawyer, accountant, engineer, appraiser or other person whose profession lends credibility to any statement used or made in support of the dividend payment.

The CBCA provides a broader due diligence defence — relieving the directors of liability if they "exercised the care, diligence and skill that a reasonably prudent person would have exercised in comparable circumstances", including reliance on this information. The due diligence defence is discussed in greater detail in Part IV.

The corporate statutes include two other significant provisions with respect to personal liability for payments to shareholders, including dividend payments. First, each director is liable for the entire amount that must be repaid to the corporation. If the other directors do not pay their share, the full amount may be extracted from just one director (this is referred to as "joint liability"). That director is, however, entitled to take action against the other directors to require them to pay their share, and against the shareholders to recover the amounts distributed to them. Second, any action taken against the directors must be taken within two years of the date on which the resolution approving the dividend was passed.

Liability for dividends and other payments made to shareholders contrary to the statute are just one example of statutory provisions that impose personal liability on directors but also provide them with a due diligence defence. Similar provisions exist in the corporate statutes in connection with the payment of an indemnity to directors and officers contrary to statutes and under securities laws in connection with misrepresentations in a prospectus.

Civil liability for secondary market disclosure

In late 2002, Ontario introduced civil liability for continuous disclosure. At the date of this printing these provisions were not yet in effect. Among other things, these provisions will allow investors to sue directors of a public company for certain written or "public oral statements" made by the corporation if those representations contain a misrepresentation.

Historically, directors have been liable to investors for misrepresentations in a prospectus, but not for misrepresentations made by the corporation in the secondary market. Since the vast majority of trades in securities occur in the secondary markets, a concern developed that directors had no incentive to be as diligent in monitoring the quality of the information released to the public as part of the corporation's continuous disclosure obligation. In the United States, investors have long been able to sue the issuers and their directors for misrepresentations in the release of information to the public or the failure to release material information on a timely basis under what is referred to as Rule "10b-5" liability in U.S. securities legislation.

These new provisions do however incorporate a number of protections for directors. Investors must obtain leave of the court before they may sue under these provisions. For many types of misrepresentation, an aggrieved investor must first satisfy a certain burden of proof and directors are able to rely on a due diligence defence.

It is not yet clear if or when the other provinces will adopt similar legislation. However, directors of corporations which are subject to Ontario securities legislation will now be well advised to adopt due diligence practices which will allow them to avoid liability under these new provisions.

S.O. 2002, c. 22, s. 185 [Not in force at date of publication].

Liability for Failing to Take All Reasonable Care

Rather than requiring directors to exercise due diligence to prevent corporations from taking certain action, some statutes require that they take "all reasonable care" to cause the corporation to take certain action. These provisions serve as incentives for directors and officers to put in place the systems and procedures necessary to enable the corporation to comply with the statutes and to monitor the operation of those systems and procedures to ensure that they continue to achieve the compliance objectives. This type of provision is found in many of the environmental protection and occupational health and safety statutes. Directors should obtain specific advice about what constitutes "all reasonable care" in respect of the particular liability. The answer often lies not only in the statute, but in what a court would find to be "industry standards" in a particular area.

LEADING DECISION

Reasonable care – the Bata decision

Bata Industries operated a shoe manufacturing plant in Batawa, Ontario. An investigation by the Ontario Ministry of the Environment revealed decay in many of the containers in which chemical wastes were stored at that plant. Some of the containers were uncovered and exposed to the elements. Ministry investigators found leaking and foaming drums and material spraying out of bung holes. There was also evidence of staining on the ground. Bata Industries, was charged with a number of offences under the *Water Resources Act* (Ontario). Three directors and officers of Bata Industries were also charged with failure to take all reasonable care to prevent a discharge. The second of these individuals was the president of Bata Industries, who was also a director. Another was the on-site manager of the division which operated the Batawa plant. The third was Thomas Bata, a director of Bata Industries and the chief executive officer of the Bata Shoe Organization (International).

The Court found the president liable on the basis that he had failed to properly supervise those responsible for environmental matters at Bata. It found that an even greater deal of blame rested with the on-site manager, because he had the authority to control his work environment, was familiar with the toxic chemicals used on the site and had been reminded of his environmental responsibilities in a memorandum from Mr. Bata.

Although Bata Industries had breached the *Water Resources Act* and two senior officers had been found liable, the Court found that Mr. Bata (a director of Bata Industries, the charged defendant) had satisfied his obligation to take all reasonable care to prevent a discharge. The Court recognized that Mr. Bata was not physically located at the Batawa site and that he functioned chiefly in an advisory capacity with respect to that aspect of the worldwide Bata operations. The Court stated that Mr. Bata was entitled to assume that the on-site manager would bring problems to his attention and that he was entitled to rely on the system of compliance he had put in place unless he became aware that the system was defective. The Court also specifically acknowledged that Mr. Bata had taken the following actions:

- he was aware of his environmental responsibilities and had written directions to that effect in a technical advisory circular sent to management;
- he personally reviewed the operation when he was on site and did not allow himself to be wilfully blind or orchestrated in his movements;
- he responded to the matters that were brought to his attention promptly and appropriately; and
- he placed an experienced manager (Mr. Weston) on site and was entitled in the circumstances to assume that Mr. Weston was addressing the environmental concerns.

R. v. Bata Industries Ltd. (1992), 7 C.E.L.R. (N.S.) 245 at 293 (Ont. Prov. Div.), varied (1993), 11 C.E.L.R. (N.S.) 208, 14 O.R. (3d) 354 (Ont. Gen. Div.), varied (1995), 18 C.E.L.R. (N.S.) 11, 25 O.R. (3d) 321 (Ont. C.A.).

INSOLVENCY RELATED LIABILITIES

Directors are subject to a number of liabilities which, practically speaking, only become relevant if the corporation is insolvent and is unable to make those payments. These provisions are generally intended to protect certain payments which the corporation is required to make — payments to employees, payments to the corporation's creditors and payments to government.

Payments to Employees

The area of liability of which directors are most acutely aware is for payments relating to the corporation's employees. Directors may be liable for unpaid wages under both the corporation's governing corporate statute and employment legislation in the jurisdictions in which it carries on business. Under most statutes, there is no due diligence defence for unpaid wages — the directors are liable if the employees are not paid for a specified period of time, in spite of any efforts they may have made to prevent that from happening. The exception is the CBCA which does offer a due diligence defence. This will be cold comfort to directors of CBCA companies, however, since they will likely also be subject to personal liability under applicable employment standards legislation in the jurisdictions in which the corporation operates.

As a corporation starts to move towards insolvency, director liability for employee wages becomes a very difficult issue. Liability may be minimized or avoided if management and the board have an opportunity to terminate employees in an orderly fashion as it becomes clear that the corporation's cash flow cannot support its current work force. This may, of course, make it more difficult for the corporation to generate cash flow and may accelerate employee severance obligations which the corporation cannot afford to meet (and for which the directors may also be liable in certain Canadian jurisdictions). Even if the corporation has been staying current with its payroll obligations, payroll cycles are almost always in arrears and it will therefore be impossible to stay completely current. Moreover, the corporation's creditors can in some cases exercise their right to take control of the corporation and shut down operations at a time when there are wages outstanding for the previous pay period. The amounts left owing to employees, and for which the directors may therefore be left personally liable, may be significant.

Liability for vacation pay under certain statutes can also be a real concern, since amounts relating to this obligation may be accrued and unpaid at the time an employee is terminated or the corporation becomes insolvent. Liability for termination and severance pay is another potentially significant cost imposed under certain statutes.

Payments to Creditors

As discussed above, explains that most corporate statutes will not allow the corporation to make payments to its shareholders (for example, by redeeming or purchasing the shareholders' shares or by paying dividends) unless certain "solvency tests" are met. Federal bankruptcy legislation also imposes liability on directors if such a payment was made within 12 months preceding its bankruptcy. Directors' diligence with respect to these matters typically includes receiving a solvency certificate from the corporation's chief financial officer. In some cases it may also be necessary to obtain a valuation of the corporation's assets. Federal bankruptcy legislation also allows a trustee in bankruptcy to apply to the court for a review of transactions that occurred in the year preceding bankruptcy in order to determine whether the transaction took place at fair market value. The court may grant judgment against the other party to the transaction and to "any other person being privy to the transaction with the bankrupt". In some cases, the directors can be held liable on the basis that they were privy to the transaction, particularly where they derived some benefit from the transaction.

Although there is relatively little case law in Canada dealing with the issue, insolvency practitioners are often concerned that directors may be exposed to claims for "trading while insolvent". This means that they could be held personally liable if they allow the corporation to purchase goods and services at a time when there is little reasonable expectation that the corporation will be able to pay for them. If the corporation stops its purchasing, the corporation may be forced into bankruptcy or restructuring proceedings. But it is not clear why directors should be expected to keep the corporation running if, by doing so, they are exposing themselves to significant personal liability.

Payments to the Government

Failure of the corporation to collect and remit to government taxes, wage and source deductions, and other tax collections may also create potential liability. Directors may be personally liable for the failure of the corporation to withhold and remit amounts relating to income tax, employment insurance and Canada Pension Plan obligations, as well as for remittance of tax collections such as GST or other value added or sales taxes, and tax withholding at source (e.g., interest paid to non-residents).

How Directors Can Protect Themselves

Directors should be vigilant in monitoring the corporation's compliance with all of its legal and contractual obligations. Just as the statutes place particular emphasis on protecting employees, creditors and government when the corporation is heading towards insolvency, so too should the directors be particularly careful to ensure that the corporation complies with the provisions protecting these parties, thereby also protecting themselves from liability.

Directors should inform themselves about due diligence defences and be satisfied that the steps necessary to establish this defence are in place, including effective monitoring procedures. These procedures should include the delivery of regular compliance statements to the board in which management confirms that all of the necessary payments are being kept current and that management knows of no reason that this will not be the case during the next period. The procedures could include regular discussions with the general counsel and chief financial officer. As is the case with any report, the directors should not accept it blindly, but should subject it to the necessary scrutiny. The nature and degree of that scrutiny will, of course, depend on the circumstances. Clearly, if a director sees the corporation's financial condition weaken, he or she should question management more closely about the contents of the compliance certificate and, perhaps, impose more stringent controls on the corporation such as establishing trust accounts into which amounts which are accruing can be placed until due.

The board should be familiar with the controls that are in place that allow management to deliver the compliance certificate. When problems come to the attention of the board as a result of their ongoing monitoring of the controls established by management, they should satisfy themselves that corrective action is being taken to rectify those problems. Records should be kept of all monitoring efforts and corrective action so that directors will be in a position to offer evidence of the action that they took in any legal proceedings.

As discussed below, there will be circumstances in which the most appropriate course of action for the directors is to resign from the board. If the corporation is being restructured under the *Bankruptcy and Insolvency Act* or the *Companies' Creditors Arrangement Act*, directors should request that the restructuring include terms protecting the directors. The initial court order under these provisions will often include an indemnity or charge on the assets of the corporation in favour of directors (and officers), usually only with respect to liabilities arising during the period following the date on which the initial order is made. This will give directors an opportunity to help guide the corporation through its financial problems, but will give them no relief against liabilities which were incurred prior to the filing. These insolvency statutes permit a proposal (or a compromise or arrangement) to include a provision for the compromise of claims (with certain exceptions) against directors of the corporation relating to obligations of the corporation. However, such protections are only available if the plan is approved and implemented.

OPPRESSION REMEDY

In Canada, certain of the corporation's stakeholders can take action against the directors (and against officers and the corporation itself) under the oppression remedy. Under this provision, if a court finds that the powers of the directors of a corporation or any of its affiliates are or have been exercised in a manner that is "oppressive or unfairly prejudicial to or that unfairly disregards the interests of any security holder, creditor, director or officer," the court may make any order it thinks fit to rectify the matters at issue. The scope of this remedy is very broad and it allows creative courts to grant a wide range of relief where they feel that it is just to do so.

The oppression remedy is available to anyone who fits within the definition of "complainant". This term clearly includes shareholders and has been found to include creditors. Generally, two factors must be present in order for the directors to be held personally liable. First, there must be some specific action or inaction on the part of the director that is directly linked to the oppressive conduct. Second, it must be appropriate for the directors to personally compensate the aggrieved party. This will be the case, for example, where directors personally benefited or furthered their control over the company through the oppressive conduct. If a director has virtually total control over the corporation (as is often the case in a private company, the shares of which are held by one person, who also acts as sole director), that director may also be held personally liable to rectify oppressive conduct on the part of the corporation.

DIRECTORS' LIABILITY FOR THEIR OWN CONDUCT
Directors can, of course, be held responsible for their own actions. The most common areas of potential liability are set out below.

Breach of Duty to the Corporation

General
The director's fiduciary duty and duty of care are discussed in Part IV above. If a director breaches one or both of these duties, he or she may be liable to the corporation for the damages caused as a result of that breach. Most corporate statutes prohibit corporations from indemnifying directors if they breached their fiduciary duty to the corporation. Many statutes also prevent the corporation from purchasing and maintaining insurance for any liability relating to the person's breach of fiduciary duty.

It seems counter-intuitive to think that the directors could be sued by the corporation if the directors are the ones who control the corporation's actions. This often creates a false sense of security on the part of directors. Two things can happen that may result in someone new making the decisions—someone who could well decide to take action against the previous board. First, if control of the corporation changes, the new controlling shareholder will likely put a new board in place. Second, if the corporation becomes insolvent and a receiver or trustee in bankruptcy steps in, the receiver or trustee will have the power to enforce any rights which the corporation has against its directors and former directors.

Derivative Action

Certain stakeholders may commence an action against the directors on behalf of the corporation through what is referred to as a "derivative action". This action could, for example, allege that the directors breached their duty to the corporation. Since the action is on behalf of the corporation, any damages which the directors are required to pay go to the corporation.

For a variety of reasons, derivative actions are not common. Under most statutes, the consent of the court is required in order for a derivative action to be commenced. Before the court will give its consent to a derivative action being commenced, it must be satisfied that the complainant is acting in good faith and in the best interests of the corporation. The person bringing the action must give the directors notice that he or she intends to bring a derivative action and give the directors the opportunity to prosecute the action themselves. The oppression remedy (discussed above) does not present any of these obstacles. In addition, a successful complainant under the oppression remedy may be able to obtain damages from the directors (rather than having those amounts paid to the corporation).

Liability in Tort

If one person injures another, the law of "tort" allows the injured person to sue the wrongdoer, subject to certain conditions. Some who feel that they have been injured by the corporation seek to recover damages not only from the corporation, but also from its directors.

The fact that the board caused the corporation to take certain action which creates a liability for the corporation does not itself give rise to personal liability for the individuals who serve as directors. However, directors, officers, and employees of a corporation remain responsible for their own conduct if it causes physical injury, property damage or nuisance, even when they were acting in the best interests of the corporation and not in their own interests. Generally, in order for an individual member of the board of directors to be held personally liable in tort as a result of some action taken by the corporation, the director must have engaged in some conduct that gives rise to an independent tort on the part of the director. Typically, he or she must have taken some action beyond taking part in decisions made by the board of directors. It should be noted that there is an exception to this rule for breach of contract. If a corporation breaches a contract with another party, the directors cannot be held liable for inducing breach of contract or for conspiring with the corporation to breach a contract. The concepts here can be a bit elusive, but it is important to note that the courts have not been prepared to allow plaintiffs to proceed against directors under tort law as a method of piercing the corporate veil.

LEADING DECISION

Liability of directors in tort – Peoples Jewellers

In the Peoples Jewellers case certain debenture holders sued both the corporation and all of its directors for misrepresentations relating to the offering of debentures. The statement of claim alleged that two of the directors (who were also officers) had attended due diligence meetings, were directly and personally involved in the marketing of the debentures and had made representations to the plaintiffs on which the plaintiffs relied. The other directors had done nothing more than authorize the transaction. The plaintiffs did not allege that those other directors had been negligent in any way. The Court permitted that action against the two directors who were actively involved to proceed to trial (it ultimately settled). The Court dismissed the action against the other directors and held that those directors could not be held vicariously liable for the negligence of the corporation.

ScotiaMcLeod Inc. v. Peoples Jewellers Ltd. (1995), 26 O.R. (3d) 481 (Ont. C.A.)

Negligent misrepresentation is one type of tort. In the *Peoples Jewellers* decision referred to above, the Court stated that it is possible for a director who made misrepresentations directly to investors to be held liable for damages suffered by an investor who relied on those misrepresentations. Similar analysis was used several years later by an Ontario court when it found that a senior officer of Dofasco Inc. had negligently misrepresented Algoma Steel's financial position to a bank in order to induce the bank to continue to extend a loan to Algoma (senior officers are generally subject to the same duties as directors). The Court said that it saw no reason to protect the senior officer from liability simply because he was acting in Dofasco's interests. Another leading case involved one corporation allegedly hiring away the employees of one of its competitors, causing the competitor significant economic damage. The competitor sued not only the corporation that had hired its employees, but one of the directors and two of the employees of that corporation who were personally involved in the recruitment program. The Court refused to dismiss the action against the three individuals and ordered that the matter proceed to trial. The Court held that the director was acting outside of his capacity as a director and could be held liable for his own tortious acts, even if he acted in the interests of the corporation. In another case, the plaintiffs named the directors and officers in an action because they stood by knowing that the plaintiff was entering into a contract with the corporation based on an incorrect understanding of relevant facts.

Liability Arising from Being an Insider

Directors are "insiders" of the corporation for the purposes of insider trading and reporting requirements.

When a person first becomes a director, he or she must report the number of securities he or she holds in the corporation within 10 days. In addition, directors (and other insiders) are required to report purchases and sales under provincial securities laws within 10 days. Insider reports are a matter of public record. These reports must now be filed (and accessed) over the Internet.

Insider trading occurs when a director (or another person in a "special relationship" with the corporation) buys or sells securities of the corporation with knowledge of a material fact or a material change which has not been generally disclosed. Prohibitions against insider trading arise under securities and corporate law and the various stock exchange rules and regulations. It is important to note that there are circumstances under which a director of a corporation can become an insider of another corporation as a result of particular transactions between the two corporations.

Securities regulators and stock exchanges are becoming increasingly vigilant and sophisticated in their enforcement of insider reporting and trading requirements. Directors of public companies need to understand and comply with their filing obligations and be sensitive to the possibility that they may have (or be perceived to have) material undisclosed information that restricts their ability to trade in securities of the corporation and that disclosure of such information to third parties may restrict such third parties from trading in securities of the corporation. The controversy surrounding Martha Stewart invited allegations that she received material inside information before she sold shares of ImClone.

A recent change by the OSC requires previously excluded transactions with banks to be reported as sales.

PART VII

How to Protect Yourself

Curiously little time seems to be spent by most directors on whether they are protected from personal liability to the fullest extent possible. Very often they simply rely on standard indemnities and insurance that have been in place for years without reviewing them in detail themselves or retaining experts to provide them with up-to-date advice.

This part of the book raises some of the issues directors should think about in order to protect themselves from liability as a result of their service to the corporation.

WHAT TO THINK ABOUT BEFORE YOU ARE SUED

The Risk of Being Sued

Being sued can be something of an occupational hazard for directors. Directors need not have done anything wrong in order to be sued. They can be named personally in actions when there may be very little prospect of imposing liability on the directors. Sometimes the plaintiff is hoping to extract a settlement from the directors' D&O insurers. In other cases, the plaintiff believes that the directors will pay more attention to and be more inclined to settle the suit if they are named themselves. If there is no merit in the lawsuit, the directors may move to have it struck out and, in some cases in Canada, the plaintiff may even be required to pay part of the costs the directors incurred in defending themselves. However, the stress of going through the process of being sued and having to fund a legal defence is significant, even if everything turns out well in the end.

While lawsuits against directors are often threatened, they may not materialize for a variety of reasons. The cost of litigating is significant and, whatever the prospects of recovery, many who feel that they have a legitimate claim may be reluctant to invest the time and money required to pursue that claim. The litigation system in Canada lends itself less readily to speculative lawsuits than does the U.S. system. Class actions are also much more difficult to commence here than they are in the United States.

Basic Protection

There are three critical issues that directors need to focus on well before there is any hint of legal action in the air. First, they need to make sure that they will have a successful defence. This defence will typically be grounded in whether directors discharged their fiduciary duty and duty of care and whether directors took the necessary steps to ensure that the corporation complied with its statutory obligations. If they are sued, directors will typically need counsel separate from the corporation's counsel. Whether all of the directors should be represented by the same counsel will depend on the facts. If a director has a different defence from the other directors, for example, it may be desirable for that director to be represented separately.

Second, they need to make sure that defence costs are not financially crippling to them. The two key concepts here are "indemnities" and "D&O insurance". When we talk about "indemnities" for a director, we generally mean the corporation's obligation to pay the director's legal expenses and, in some cases, any fine or judgment the director is required to pay. D&O insurance is "directors' and officers' insurance", which the corporation purchases from an insurance company. If appropriate indemnities and insurance are in place, directors may be able to avoid paying significant out-of-pocket costs in defending themselves

Directors need to have copies of their D&O insurance and all indemnities under which they may be able to make a claim. There is no way to know what a director's relationship with the corporation will be at the time when he or she needs to rely on the indemnity or insurance. In some cases, the corporation may not itself have kept complete files and will therefore not be able to provide directors with the necessary documents when it becomes critical.

Finally, they should also know when resigning from the board it is the only protection left. This will happen only in extreme cases and will often involve the resignation of the entire board on the advice of counsel.

INDEMNITIES

Under certain circumstances, the corporate statutes require that the corporation indemnify its directors for the costs they incur in being sued. Directors have a right to indemnification from the corporation in certain circumstances under most corporate statutes. This generally means that, if the director is sued in his or her capacity as a director, the corporation will reimburse the director for legal expenses and other amounts the director is required to pay in connection with the lawsuit.

The legal landscape with respect to directors' indemnities is quite complicated and very technical. This section of the book sorts through this morass by setting out the basic framework of indemnities and then providing additional details on each important element of this framework.

Basic Framework

The provisions in most of the corporate statutes can be distilled to the following four points:

1) The corporation is required by statute to indemnify a director who has been sued and has successfully defended the action, subject to certain restrictions.

2) Even if the director does not successfully defend the action, the corporation may indemnify him or her, subject to certain restrictions.

3) There are special rules if the director is sued pursuant to a "derivative action", i.e., an action by a shareholder or creditor (or some other person contemplated by the statute) on behalf of the corporation.

4) Directors can be made personally liable for an indemnity which the corporation pays to another director if that payment is contrary to the statute.

When Does the Statute Require the Corporation to Indemnify?

Under most of the corporate statutes, a corporation is required to indemnify a director who was "substantially successful on the merits in defending the action or proceeding." In other words, the director must first have won the lawsuit. Then, two further conditions must be satisfied. First, the director must have acted "honestly and in good faith, with a view to the best interests of the corporation." In other words, the director must have acted in a manner consistent with his or her fiduciary duty with respect to the action or matter for which the director is seeking indemnification. Second, the director must have had reasonable grounds for believing that his or her conduct was lawful. (The test in the CBCA now is that the director must not have been found by the court to have committed any fault or omitted to do anything that he or she should have done.)

These provisions raise a number of issues, none of which has been addressed by the case law. There are also a number of very technical deficiencies in the indemnity provisions of the corporate statutes which could present serious issues for directors seeking to rely on their provisions. Directors should have an understanding of these deficiencies and ensure, to the extent possible, that they obtain other indemnities (from the corporation or others) that supplement the indemnity from the corporation.

Indemnities Beyond What the Statute Provides

Most corporations provide their directors with indemnities beyond what is provided for in the statute. In part, this reflects a recognition that a corporation will not be able to attract talented individuals to its board and management team if it is not prepared to protect them from the liabilities to which they are exposed in serving the corporation.

The additional indemnity which most corporations provide is a routine provision in the corporation's by-laws. Often it is given very little thought by the corporation or the directors. In most cases, this by-law provision could be improved. However, it would also be desirable for most directors to obtain a separate contractual indemnity from the corporation. Both of these approaches to indemnification are discussed.

By-Law Indemnities

In Canada, it is common for the corporation to provide an indemnity for its directors in its by-laws. Although there is no requirement governing how the by-law provision should read, in most cases, it simply mirrors the language of the corporate statutes. In other words, the by-law requires the corporation to indemnify the directors to the extent permitted by the corporate statutes, provided that they were not in breach of their fiduciary duty and they believed what they were doing was lawful.

While it is important for the directors that there be an indemnity in the by-laws, the language in the by-laws should be reviewed carefully on behalf of the directors to improve the language taken from the statute. Directors should be aware that an amendment to the by-laws to add or revise an indemnity in favour of the directors requires shareholder approval. It may therefore be difficult to amend these provisions to respond to changing circumstances. Further, since the by-law is not a contract between the director or officer and the corporation, an individual director or officer cannot control whether the indemnity in a by-law is revised or even eliminated. For these reasons, directors should carefully consider obtaining a contractual indemnity as well.

Contractual Indemnities

It is wise for directors to have a contractual indemnity from the corporation, in addition to any indemnity provided in the by-laws or under the corporate statute. This is a contract between the director and the corporation. It is usually a short document, running from a couple of pages to 10 pages or more, depending on how detailed it is. Usually, the corporation cannot change this agreement or terminate it without the directors' consent. A contractual indemnity can be used to clarify ambiguities in the language of the corporate statute and address gaps in the statute and add certain implementing details not included in the statute.

A director should also consider who might provide an indemnity other than the corporation. For example, it is often wise to supplement the protection afforded by an indemnity from the corporation with an indemnity from the controlling shareholder or from a subsidiary of the corporation that has significant assets. There must generally be some reason for the other person to be entering into the indemnity or it may not be enforceable (on the basis that no "consideration" passed from the director to the other person). However, in many cases, it will be in the interest of the person providing the indemnity to secure or retain the services of the director and there may therefore be a sufficient basis on which the person can provide an enforceable indemnity.

Are You Covered?

Two factors must be considered to determine whether a person is covered by the indemnity provisions of most corporate statutes (and by the customary provisions in the corporation's by-laws). The first is the person's relationship to the corporation. The second is the nature of the event which gives rise to the need for indemnification.

Whom Does the Indemnity Cover?

The indemnity provisions in most corporate statutes apply to directors and officers of a corporation — both those currently in office and those who served as directors or officers in the past. This is important since many liabilities may continue after an individual resigns as an officer or director and may be enforced for a period of time after a resignation. An individual who was on the board at the time the event occurred can be held liable for the specified period of time, even after he or she has subsequently left the board.

The indemnity provisions of most corporate statutes will typically also cover a director if he or she serves on certain other boards at the request of the corporation. Before agreeing to serve on the board of a subsidiary, joint venture, partnership, or any other entity in which the corporation has an interest, a director should be very clear about whether he or she will be covered by indemnities that are already in place and whether additional indemnities are desirable (whether from the parent corporation specifically covering the new exposure or from the subsidiary itself).

When Does the Indemnity Apply?

The indemnification provisions of most of the corporate statutes apply if the director was "made a party" to an action or proceeding as a result of being a director. There is serious doubt about whether these provisions would cover legal costs incurred by a director in connection with a regulatory investigation, since an investigation is not an "action or proceeding". Even if there is an action or proceeding, the director will not be covered unless he or she is actually named in that action or proceeding. This is one of the most problematic aspects of the statutory provision, since it is often wise for the directors to retain counsel (and therefore to incur costs for which they will wish to seek indemnification) when the corporation is under investigation. This deficiency in the corporate statutes has been addressed in the recent amendments to the CBCA, but still exists in most other corporate statutes.

Derivative Action

Most of the corporate statutes have different provisions dealing with indemnities in the case of a derivative action. Typically, they provide that if a director or officer seeks an indemnity with respect to a derivative action or an action brought by the corporation, he or she must obtain the approval of the court. This requirement seeks to prevent the very people the corporation is suing from causing the corporation to pay their costs and expenses. A corporation may, with court approval, indemnify a director or officer in a derivative action who meets the requirements for a permitted indemnity.

What Items Are Covered?

The amounts that are covered by the statutory provisions are referred to in the statutes as "costs, charges and expenses" and are specifically stated to include an amount paid to settle an action or satisfy a judgment. The costs, charges and expenses for which a director seeks indemnification must have been "reasonably incurred" by the person. Most corporate statutes expressly authorize a corporation to indemnify a director or officer in the case of a criminal or administrative action or proceeding that is enforced by a monetary penalty if he or she had reasonable grounds for believing that his or her conduct was lawful. On its face, this language should permit corporations to indemnify qualifying directors or officers for fines because they are "amounts paid to satisfy a judgment" or "costs, charges and expenses" incurred in respect of criminal or administrative actions or proceedings.

The indemnification provisions of most corporate statutes refer to costs "incurred". They would therefore include legal fees (provided they were reasonable) as well as penalties and fines. They may also include travel and other out-of-pocket costs, again, provided that they were reasonable.

Some Issues to Consider

The statutory and customary by-law provisions relating to indemnities do not provide directors with complete protection. Directors and corporations should turn their minds to the appropriate scope of protection rather than relying on statutory provisions and the customary documents in this critical area.

There will obviously be tension between the interests of the director and the interests of the corporation in negotiating an indemnity. The corporation wants to attract and retain good directors but should also want to limit the basis on which it might be required to provide an indemnity. The directors want as complete an indemnity as the law will allow for themselves personally. At the same time, however, directors can be held personally liable for approving an indemnity contrary to the provisions of the statute and will not want to be exposed to this liability in connection with an indemnity paid to other directors.

Directors should consider having the following issues dealt with in their indemnity agreement:

- The costs, charges and expenses for which the director is covered should include legal and other professional fees and out-of-pocket expenses for attending discoveries, trials, hearings and meetings to prepare for those proceedings.

- The indemnity should cover investigations, inquiries and hearings, whether or not charges have been laid against the corporation or the director.
- The director should be entitled to full indemnification notwithstanding any deductible amounts or policy limits contained in the D&O insurance policy.
- The indemnity should apply when the director is compelled by authorities or requested by the corporation to participate in the action or proceeding.
- It should be clear who will have carriage of the director's defence, who will engage and instruct legal counsel and who decides when legal representation is required (i.e., the corporation or the director).
- If the corporation has D&O insurance, the director should be indemnified promptly, rather than being required to wait for indemnification until the corporation has received the insurance proceeds.
- The indemnity should provide for immediate and full payment of the director's legal defence costs as actually incurred until it is determined that the cause of action being defended is neither indemnifiable nor insured.
- In the event of a dispute, the corporation or director, at the corporation's expense, will make application to the court to approve the indemnity.
- The indemnity should survive indefinitely following a director who ceases to be a director.

Director Liability for Indemnity Payments

Under most of the corporate statutes, directors who vote for or consent to a resolution authorizing an indemnity payment contrary to the statute are jointly and severally liable to restore to the corporation any unrecovered amounts. For example, authorizing indemnification for a director who breached his or her fiduciary duty would be contrary to the statute and would accordingly attract personal liability for the directors who approved that indemnity.

An action under this provision must be brought two years from the date of the resolution authorizing the payment of the indemnity.

There is a due diligence defence comparable to the due diligence defence described in Part IV with respect to the payment of dividends.

Disclosure

Under most corporate statutes, if indemnification pursuant to the statute is paid or becomes payable in the financial period, a corporation that is required to send a management proxy circular must disclose such payment in the circular. It must disclose the amount paid or payable, the name and title of the individual indemnified or to be indemnified, and the circumstances that gave rise to the indemnity.

D&O INSURANCE

General

"D&O insurance" can offer protection to both the corporation and to its directors and officers. From the corporation's perspective, D&O insurance helps to manage the risk that the corporation may be required to pay out under such an indemnity. From the directors' perspective, D&O insurance will often be desirable to protect against situations where an indemnity from the corporation may not be available or sufficient. In addition, any indemnity is only as good as the financial strength of the corporation giving it. If a corporation experiences financial difficulties, it may be unable to honour its indemnity. Coverage under a D&O policy is unaffected by the corporation's financial condition as long as the premiums are paid.

Approving D&O Insurance

The board of directors is very often involved in the decision to acquire D&O insurance (although the decision is sometimes made by officers of the corporation). Directors will obviously want the widest possible coverage for the specific risks encountered in the conduct of the corporation's business. They should bear in mind that it may be in the corporation's interests to minimize insurance premiums and the corporation may be prepared to agree to exclusions, coverage limitations, deductibles, policy dollar limits and other endorsements (i.e., restrictions on) to the insurance. The decision to purchase and maintain D&O insurance, like any other decision, must be made in a manner that is consistent with the fiduciary duty and duty of care imposed on those responsible for the decision.

In deciding whether to purchase D&O insurance, the costs and benefits to the corporation, including the following, must be considered:

- The cost of insurance. The size of the premiums will depend on a number of factors, including the size of the corporation, the nature of its business, the industry in which it operates and the corporation's past experience.
- The scope of the coverage, including the amount for deductibles and the policy limits. For example, the policy may exclude coverage for the risks that are of the greatest concern to the directors and officers (such as liability for environmental matters) and be totally inadequate for the amount of potential claims (such as the Enron claims).
- The likelihood that any director or officer would ultimately claim against the insurance. For example, derivative actions are relatively rare in Canada (in contrast to the United States). A board might conclude that it cannot justify the cost of insuring against a relatively remote risk.
- The need to provide insurance to attract and retain highly qualified board members and senior managers.

Statutory Limits on Insurance

Many corporate statutes prohibit the corporation from purchasing D&O insurance against a breach of fiduciary duty. This limitation was recently removed from the CBCA.

The Standard D&O Policy

Directors' and officers' liability insurance is negotiated between the corporation and the insurer using a standard form policy as the starting point. A corporation should retain an experienced insurance professional to assist it in obtaining the best available insurance coverage. It should also consider retaining legal counsel to help it identify the risks to which its directors and officers are exposed and to review the policy before it is settled.

Directors should be familiar with any D&O policy the corporation is proposing to buy. Prospective directors should review the insurance policy before joining a board to avoid discovering, just when they seek to rely on the policy, that the very liabilities they are most worried about are the ones excluded from the policy.

The insurance application is critical. A director will be asked to provide certain information and it will be critical that the director do whatever background work is necessary in order to be able to provide accurate information. The insurer relies on the information provided to it in the application and, if those statements are shown to be incorrect, this could ultimately lead to lack of coverage. Directors should be concerned that their own coverage will not be compromised if the corporation or another director provides incorrect information to the insurer. A severability clause in the contract will provide that the insurance application is a separate application by each insured person and that the statements of knowledge of one director will not be seen as the statements or knowledge of another.

Once the policy is in place, directors should be familiar with their ongoing obligations under the policy. For example, there is typically a requirement that insured persons notify the insurer of any material changes as soon as practicable. The policy may subsequently not respond if the insured fails to do so. Directors should be familiar with the definitions of "loss", "wrongful act" and the exclusions under the policy so that they will understand the scope of the policy.

Directors should be aware that D&O coverage is typically offered on a "claims made" basis — in other words, coverage is triggered by claims made against the directors and officers during the policy period, typically for wrongful acts committed before or during the policy period. Policies are typically renewed annually. Insurers may resist renewing the policy when the corporation is in financial difficulty, but if formal restructuring proceedings are underway, a court may be prepared to order the insurer to continue coverage provided that premiums continue to be paid.

Extended policy periods are available under most policies — for an additional premium. Coverage can be obtained for wrongful acts committed before or during the policy period, but discovered after the policy period expires. Directors should ensure that they are familiar with these provisions and, where necessary, will be in a position to pay the additional premium themselves if the corporation is unable or unwilling to do so.

Insurance will very often cover the corporation and its subsidiaries — this will likely mean that directors will also be covered if they are asked to sit on the board of a subsidiary. However, it may also mean that, if a subsidiary runs into serious difficulty, legal proceedings affecting only the directors of the subsidiary corporation may drain all of the coverage under the policy, leaving nothing available for directors of the parent company board or the directors of any other subsidiary corporation.

WHEN TO RESIGN

Resignation will of course limit a director's exposure to liability to some extent. For example, a director will only be liable for actions that occurred while he or she was actually on the board. Further, under certain of the statutory provisions imposing liability on directors, directors can only be sued for a period of years after they cease to be directors. Accordingly, resignation will begin the limitation period for these liabilities. Directors can, of course, also save themselves a considerable amount of anguish and time by leaving a board when a firm appears to be headed for bankruptcy; however, this is a decision that should be taken only after a great deal of thought and consultation with legal counsel.

Directors have a well-defined fiduciary duty to the company. Clearly, these duties and obligations should not be abandoned at the first sign of trouble. Most directors will feel that they have a moral, if not a legal obligation, to do everything they can to save the enterprise and to protect to the fullest extent possible the interests of the stakeholders. To walk away when the situation becomes difficult, rather than attempting to solve the problems, is impossible for many.

At some point, it will become clear that there is no equity left in the enterprise and that any assets effectively belong to the creditors. In the past few years, jurisprudence has developed, particularly in the United States, which rules that the directors' fiduciary duty, when there is no equity left for shareholders, flows to the creditors. To the extent that similar jurisprudence develops in Canada, all directors must be extremely careful because at some point they must begin to direct their efforts not to saving the company for the owners, but rather to maximizing returns for the creditors. Exactly when that point arises is very difficult to determine.

Once it is clear that there is no equity left for the shareholders, all the statutory obligations have been provided for and the creditors are clearly in charge, then directors may resign with a clear conscience. After all, they were elected by the shareholders and the interests of the shareholders are now minimal. Consequently, if the board is to stay, it should do so only if it has the full support of the creditors. Such support may best be ascertained by determining whether or not creditors are willing to advance funds to keep the enterprise alive. In most instances, they will not and since at that point the creditors own all the existing assets of the company, the board could in good faith consider resigning.

If directors decide to resign because of concern with management, they should consider whether shareholders and the investing public are entitled to be made aware of their concerns. If no one knows why the resignation has occurred, it will not have been effective.

PART VIII

Technical Underpinnings

STATUTORY AND REGULATORY FRAMEWORK

The basic corporate governance framework is set out in the corporate statutes, supplemented (in the case of public companies) by securities regulation and (in the case of listed companies) by stock exchange requirements and other best practices guidelines. This part of the book gives those readers with an interest a more detailed and technical explanation of these matters.

The Statutes That Create the Corporation

In Canada, a corporation can be formed under the CBCA, or under the business corporations or companies acts of one of Canada's 10 provinces or three territories. Most of the provincial and territorial statutes are similar to the CBCA, although each contains some significant differences. The exceptions are the corporate statutes in Nova Scotia, Prince Edward Island, British Columbia and Quebec:

- Nova Scotia and British Columbia are "memorandum of association" jurisdictions. The significance of this from a governance perspective is that many of the governance requirements enshrined in the CBCA and similar statutes are set out instead in the memorandum of association, with the result that the shareholders are able to change the company's governance structure to a much greater extent than is possible under the CBCA. British Columbia's *Company Act* has evolved into a hybrid of the memorandum of association approach and the approach used in the CBCA, having incorporated into the statute many of the basic governance provisions in the CBCA and similar statutes. A company's memorandum of association is filed with the applicable government office when the company is formed, just as articles of incorporation are filed when a CBCA corporation is formed.

- Prince Edward Island is a letters patent jurisdiction. Its corporate statute contains very little in the way of governance provisions.

- Quebec is a civil law jurisdiction, in contrast to all other Canadian jurisdictions, which are common law based. While the approach to governance in the *Companies Act* (Quebec) and the *Civil Code of Quebec* is similar to that found in the CBCA and similar statutes, there are necessarily differences that arise as a result of a different legal regime and legislative approach.

Not-for-profit corporations are generally formed under a statute that provides for non-share capital corporations. A non-share capital corporation has members rather than shareholders and the members are not entitled to the profits earned by the corporation. These statutes are infrequently amended and accordingly many of their governance provisions will seem to be quite out of date when compared with the CBCA-style statutes. The federal non-share capital statute has been subject to study and an extensive consultation process. As a result, it is in the process of being amended and updated.

Public sector corporations, including Crown corporations, are typically created by special acts of parliament. They often include their own governance regime—at least in part. Typically, for example, they will provide for the appointment of directors and certain basic duties and standards of conduct on the part of directors. Other aspects of the governance regime, such as conflict of interest and indemnification provisions, are often incorporated by reference from the corporate statute of the applicable jurisdiction.

References in this book to the provisions of the corporate statutes are generally references to the statutory provisions in the CBCA-style statutes.

Securities Laws

Securities regulation is a matter of provincial jurisdiction in Canada, although the various provincial and territorial regulators engage in varying degrees of co-operation (depending on the issue) to co-ordinate their regulation of the Canadian capital markets. Discussions in various quarters are continuing about how to streamline securities regulations in Canada—whether through a national securities commission or uniform securities laws. References in this book to securities laws are generally references to Ontario securities laws.

Regulation of corporate governance has generally been left to the corporate statutes, with very little in the way of governance requirements in securities law statutes. The first significant departure from this division of jurisdiction is now OSC Rule 61-501 (and its Quebec counterpart, Policy 27), which prescribes certain governance standards in connection with specific types of transactions which inherently involve potential conflicts of interest. The transactions currently covered by this policy are:

- insider bids—a take-over bid by an insider (such as an officer, director or holder of 10% or more of the shares of the corporation)
- issuer bids—an offer by the corporation to acquire shares from its shareholders (with certain exceptions, such as shares that are redeemable on their terms)
- going-private transactions—a transaction which requires certain shareholders to give up their "participating securities", such as common shares
- related party transactions—a transaction between the corporation and any person who is a "related party", which includes an officer, director or holder of 10% or more of the shares of the corporation.

Several years ago, the OSC began making rules affecting areas of an issuer's governance which were not previously covered in Canadian securities laws. One example is the requirement that the board review the corporation's interim financial statements before they are released. More recently, securities laws in Ontario have been amended to give the OSC rule-making authority with respect to audit committees. Proposed rules with respect to the composition and responsibilities of audit committees of reporting issuers have now been released (See "June 2003 Update").

Stock Exchanges

In Canada, senior issuers are listed on the TSX and junior issuers are listed on the TSX Ventures Exchange — either as Tier 1 or Tier 2 companies. In order to obtain a listing on either of these exchanges, an issuer must satisfy a number of criteria, including having a minimum "public float", being:

- for a TSX listing, at least 1 million freely tradeable shares with a market value of at least $4 million held by at least 300 public holders, each holding a board lot (i.e., 100 shares)
- for a listing as a Tier 1 company on the TSX Ventures Exchange, at least 1 million freely tradeable shares with a market value of at least $1 million held by at least 300 public holders, each holding a board lot (i.e., 100 shares), with at least 20% of the shares in the hands of the public
- for a listing as a Tier 2 company on the TSX Ventures Exchange, at least 500,000 freely tradeable shares with a market value of at least $500,000 held by at least 300 public holders, each holding a board lot (i.e., 100 shares), with at least 20% of the shares in the hands of the public.

Both the TSX and the TSX Venture Exchange impose certain governance requirements on listed companies (such as requiring shareholder approval for certain transactions) and require that a listed company obtain their consent before it may proceed with certain transactions. In addition, the TSX requires listed companies incorporated in Canada to provide their shareholders with certain disclosure about their governance practices each year.

References in this book to stock exchange requirements are generally references to the requirements of the TSX.

CONSTATING DOCUMENTS/CHARTER DOCUMENTS

The articles of incorporation and by-laws of a corporation (and, in some private companies, a unanimous shareholder agreement) are often referred to as the corporation's "constating documents" or the "charter documents". Each of these is discussed in more detail below.

Articles

General

A corporation's articles (meaning the articles of incorporation and any amendments to those articles) set out the following:

- the corporation's name
- where the registered office is situated
- the classes of shares that the corporation is authorized to issue (and any maximum number of shares it is authorized to issue)
- the share conditions attaching to each class of shares
- any restrictions on the issue, transfer or ownership of the shares
- the number of directors (or, in some cases, the minimum and maximum number of directors)
- any restrictions on the business.

The articles may also include other provisions overriding certain of the statutory provisions which would apply in the absence of anything contained in the articles. For example, under most corporate statutes, the articles may contain restrictions on the authority of directors to issue shares, redeem shares, borrow money, delegate to officers and fix their own remuneration or that of officers or employees (in addition to a number of other matters).

Share Conditions

As noted above, the articles must include the share conditions attaching to each class of the corporation's shares. There is a great deal of flexibility about what may be included in share conditions. However, the shares of a corporation carry three basic rights:

1) the right to vote at any meeting of shareholders (including to elect directors) and to appoint auditors;

2) the right to receive any dividend declared by the corporation; and

3) the right to receive the remaining property of the corporation upon dissolution (after all the creditors have been paid).

One class of shares may have all of these rights (as common shares typically do). Another class of shares (often preference shares) may also have some or all of these rights, often in various combinations and permutations. Preference shares will often be non-voting, with specified dividends and a priority right to a return of the capital invested if the corporation is dissolved. In some cases, a right to vote for directors may arise only if their dividends have not been paid for a prescribed period of time.

Securities laws and stock exchanges may impose certain requirements on what a class of shares may be called (for example, restricted voting shares must be designated as such). They may also require that certain provisions be included in the corporation's articles under certain circumstances (such as provisions referred to as "coattails" to protect certain shareholders in the event of a take-over bid).

By-Laws

By-laws are rules adopted by the corporation, setting out certain aspects of the way in which it will be governed. Very often a corporation's by-laws repeat (and to the extent permitted modify) the governance provisions of the applicable corporate statute, in order to consolidate in one place all of the requirements relating to the corporation's governance. The by-laws will often go on to provide more detailed provisions relating to certain matters, such as the conduct of meetings of shareholders and directors.

By-laws must be approved by the corporation's shareholders. While the board has the authority to make, amend or repeal any by-law, this is only effective until the next meeting of shareholders and then, only if it is ratified at that meeting.

Unanimous Shareholder Agreement

Unanimous shareholder agreements are discussed in Part II. The agreements provide a basis on which shareholders may change the most fundamental aspect of the governance structure set out in most corporate statutes — the authority of the board of directors to manage or supervise the management of the business and affairs of the corporation. By signing a unanimous shareholder agreement, shareholders can take some or all of that authority from the directors and exercise it themselves.

One of the most frequently asked questions about unanimous shareholder agreements is whether directors are relieved of all liability for those matters for which their authority has been removed pursuant to a unanimous shareholder agreement. Although the corporate statutes provide that shareholders who restrict the directors' powers thereby assume the directors' liabilities to the same extent, other statutes that specifically impose liability on directors generally do not include this provision and the courts have not provided any comfort on this point. However, it seems very unlikely that a court would be prepared to make a director liable for conduct by the corporation over which the director had no control.

Unanimous shareholder agreements have sometimes been used to try to protect individuals from liability in their role as directors by having the responsibilities and liabilities of the board of directors vested in a corporate shareholder. The effectiveness of this kind of liability shield for directors has not been tested before the courts.

BEST PRACTICE GUIDELINES

Major Canadian Reports and Publications

There has been significant evolution in corporate governance standards and practices in Canada in the last 10 years — almost all of which has come through reports and voluntary codes of governance best practice rather than through legislative or regulatory change. The leading reports are:

- The Dey Report — The Report of the Toronto Stock Exchange Committee on Corporate Governance in Canada released in

1994. The TSX Guidelines (discussed below) were drawn from the best practice guidelines recommended in the Dey Report.

- Five Years to the Dey — Report on Corporate Governance sponsored by the Institute of Corporate Directors and the TSX in 1999. This report sets out the results of a survey of the state of corporate governance among TSX-listed companies in the five-year period following the release of the Dey Report.
- The State of Governance In Canada — the Report of the Reunion Meeting of the Dey Committee, sponsored by the Institute of Corporate Directors and the TSX and held in April 2000. This document reports on the discussions of the members of the Dey Committee on the developments in corporate governance in Canada since their report was released in late 1994.
- Saucier Report — The Report of the Joint Committee on Corporate Governance in Canada released in November 2001. The work of the Saucier Committee was jointly sponsored by the Canadian Institute of Chartered Accountants, the TSX and TSX Venture Exchange (then CDNX). It recommended certain changes to the TSX Guidelines, which are currently under consideration by the TSX.
- Report of the Five Year Review Committee established by the Ministry of Finance to review the *Securities Act* (Ontario).
- Governance Values and Competitiveness — A Commitment to Leadership, A Report of the Council of Chief Executives.

There have been a number of important books written on Canadian corporate governance. These include:
- James Gillies, *Boardroom Renaissance: Power, Morality and Performance in Modern Corporations*. McGraw-Hill Ryerson Limited, 1992.
- David S.R. Leighton and Donald H. Thain, *Making Boards Work: What Directors Must do to Make Canadian Boards Effective*. McGraw-Hill Ryerson Limited, 1997.
- William A. Dimma, *Excellence in the Boardroom: Best Practices in Corporate Directorship*. Wiley, 2002.
- John Carver with Caroline Oliver, *Corporate Boards That Create Value: Governing Company Performance from the Boardroom*. Jossey-Bass, 2002.

- Maureen J. Sabia and James L. Goodfellow, *Integrity in the Spotlight: Opportunities for Audit Committees*. The Canadian Institute of Chartered Accountants, 2002.

The Canadian Institute of Chartered Accountants makes a significant contribution to corporate governance provided to directors. In February it published *Strategic Planning: What Boards Should Expect from CFOs*. It has also created a series of Boardroom Briefings which include:
- *20 Questions Directors Should Ask About Risk.*
- *20 Questions Directors Should Ask About Strategy.*
- *20 Questions Directors Should Ask About Executive Compensation.*
- *20 Questions Directors Should Ask About Management's Discussion and Analysis.*
- *20 Questions Directors Should Ask About Pension Accountability.*

There are also a number of reports released annually which are followed closely by the Canadian business community, the most recent of which have been:
- *Corporate Board Governance and Director Compensation in Canada: A View of 2002*. Patrick O'Callagan & Associations in Partnership with Korn/Ferry International (December 2002).
- *Spencer Stuart Board Index Report* (11th annual report, October 2002).

TSX Guidelines

The TSX Guidelines set out the 14 best practice corporate governance guidelines recommended in the Dey Report in 1994. In 2001, the Saucier Report recommended certain amendments to the TSX Guidelines. The TSX released certain proposed amendments for comment early in 2002, only to pull them back for reconsideration after the enactment of Sarbanes-Oxley. The TSX proposed amendments were revised following the release of Sarbanes-Oxley and sent to the OSC for comment in November 2002. Those proposals are expected to be released for public comment later in 2003.

Under its corporate governance policy, both as currently in effect and when modified by the proposed amendments, the TSX requires Canadian companies with shares listed on the TSX to disclose on an annual basis, either in their proxy circular or in their annual report, whether their governance practices align with the practices recommended in the TSX Guidelines. The proposed amendments would also introduce certain corporate governance listing requirements for the first time, including the requirements to have an audit committee.

Guidelines from Canadian Institutional Investors

There are a number of institutional investors and other organizations in Canada that develop and publish guidelines setting out their view of corporate governance standards. For example, the Pension Investment Association of Canada maintains Corporate Governance Standards, which are used by many of Canada's pension funds in evaluating the governance practices of the corporations in which they invest. In addition, some of Canada's largest institutional investors (including the Ontario Teachers' Pension Plan Board, Ontario Municipal Employees Retirement Board, Caisse de Dépôt et placement du Québec, B.C. Investment Management Corporation, and the Canada Pension Plan Investment Board) publish proxy voting guidelines, setting out how they intend to vote in respect of particular governance matters. These guidelines have significantly influenced governance practices.

In addition, certain Canadian organizations have had significant influence in establishing best practices, in particular the Institute of Corporate Directors and The Canadian Institute of Chartered Accountants.

U.S. Best Practices

Canadian corporations and regulators monitor governance developments in other jurisdictions (particularly the United States). The work of the Blue Ribbon Commission on Improving the Effectiveness of Audit Committees released in 1999 was particularly influential. Most recently the New York Stock Exchange Corporate Accountability and Listings Standards Committee recommended the introduction of a number of corporate governance practices, compliance with which would become a condition of listing on the NYSE.

Other influential publications include:

- the American Law Institute's Principles of Corporate Governance: Analysis and Recommendations;
- the Business Roundtable's Principles of Corporate Governance (2002) and its earlier Statement on Corporate Governance (1997);
- the various Blue Ribbon Commission Reports published by the National Association of Corporate Directors.
- Report of the Conference Board Commission on Public Trust and Private Enterprise (2003).

As is the case in Canada, U.S. institutional investors publish their own best practice codes. Among these, the most well known are the codes published by the California Public Employees' Retirement System (CalPERS), Teachers Insurance and Annuity Association — College Retirement Fund (TIAA-CREF), and by the Council of Institutional Investors (CII).

Other International Developments

Efforts to promote good corporate governance have been ongoing around the world for the last decade. The first of the major reports was the Cadbury Report, released in the United Kingdom in 1992. The work of the Cadbury Committee was followed by a report of the Greenbury Committee in 1995 and the Hampel Committee in 1998. The recommendations from these three reports have been combined into the current code of best practice, called the "Combined Code", which now falls under the Financial Services Authority in the United Kingdom.

Transnational examples include the OECD Principles of Corporate Governance issued by the Organisation for Economic Cooperation and Development and the Principles for Corporate Governance in the Commonwealth (also known as the CACG Guidelines), both issued in 1999.

In January 2003, the Higgs Report and the Smith Report were both released. It is anticipated that their recommendations will lead to changes in the Combined Code. The Higgs Report deals with the role and effectiveness of non-executive directors. It recommends a greater proportion of independent, better-informed individuals on the board, greater transparency and accountability in the board-room, formal performance appraisals and a more rigorous appointments process. It also calls for closer relationships between non-executive directors and shareholders. The Smith Report sets out the key elements of the audit committee's role, focusing on the auditor's independence and maintaining the integrity of the company's financial statements.

Stock exchanges, securities regulators and governmental bodies in a number of other countries have also commissioned corporate governance studies. These reports have led, in some cases, to the adoption of best practice codes by stock exchanges and, in other cases, to the adoption of corporate governance requirements by legislatures and regulators.

Glossary

AIF Annual information form with detailed information on the corporation's background, operations, management and nature of its business and capital structure which is filed with securities regulators (applicable only to reporting issuers)

Articles of Incorporation Document filed with the appropriate government office to form a corporation. The corporate statutes of some jurisdictions provide for a memorandum of association (Nova Scotia and BC) or letters patent (PEI) rather than articles of incorporation

Audit Committee Financial Expert A term used in the SEC rule implementing section 407 of Sarbanes-Oxley that issuers disclose whether there is a "financial expert" on the audit committee

BIA *Bankruptcy and Insolvency Act* (Canada)

By-Laws Rules dealing with the governance of the corporation, adopted by the corporation (in most cases approved by the board and then ratified by the shareholders)

CBCA *Canada Business Corporation Act.* This is the federal corporate law statute. Each of the provinces and territories also have a corporate law statute. Generally, one can choose where to incorporate and accordingly which statute will govern the corporation

CEO Chief executive officer, the most senior member of management, reporting directly to the board of directors. Typically the CEO is a member of the board of directors

Charter Documents Under most Canadian statutes, the articles of incorporation (or Letters Patent or Articles of Association), the by-laws and the unanimous shareholder agreement, if there is one. Also known as constating documents

Constating Documents (see Charter Documents)

CICA Canadian Institute of Chartered Accountants

Common Law Law based solely on the authority of the courts (as distinguished from law created by statute)

Derivative Actions A legal action by a shareholder or other party on behalf of the corporation

Dey Report *Where Were the Directors? – Guidelines for Improved Corporate Governance in Canada,* Report of the Toronto Stock Exchange Committee on Corporate Governance in Canada released in December 1994

D&O Insurance Directors and officers liability insurance, typically purchased by the corporation from a third party insurer

Derivative Actions A legal action by a shareholder or other party on behalf of the corporation

Enron Enron Corp., a Houston-based energy company that filed for bankruptcy in the fall of 2001

Financial Expert A term currently used in the NYSE and Nasdaq corporate governance listing requirements to describe a member of an audit committee who has had professional experience in preparing financial statements. Sarbanes-Oxley also refers to "financial experts", although that term was changed by the SEC in its rules implementing certain of the provisions of Sarbanes-Oxley to "audit committee financial expert"

Financial Literacy A term coined by the NACD and now used by the NYSE and Nasdaq in their corporate governance listing requirements (and by the TSX in the proposed amendments to the TSX Guidelines) to describe the ability of a director to read and understand financial statements

GAAP Generally accepted accounting principles. In this book, the term "GAAP" means Canadian GAAP – the United States and many other jurisdictions have their own "generally accepted accounting principles" which are also referred to as "GAAP"

GAAS Generally accepted auditing standards. GAAS sets out standards relating to the auditor's qualifications, the performance of the auditor's examination and the preparation of the auditor's report. In this book, the term "GAAS" means Canadian GAAS

ICD[*] Institute of Corporate Directors (www.icd.ca), an organization with chapters across Canada focusing on corporate governance issues in Canada

Indemnity Agreement to pay any amount which the person having the benefit of the indemnity is required to pay

Independent Director This term has a formal meaning in Canada only in the context of OSC Rule 61-501 (and QSC Policy 27), where it is used in the context of certain types of transactions. Otherwise, the term is used loosely in Canada either to refer to directors who have no relationship with management or to refer to directors who have no relationship either with management or with a significant shareholder

Information Circular Information sent to shareholders with management's request for shareholder's voting proxy along with the annual audited financial reports, sometimes called a "proxy circular"

Insider This is a technical term that has a specific meaning for corporate and securities law purposes. It is intended to capture relationships with the corporation in which people are likely to have information about the corporation which is not generally available. Directors are always insiders of the corporation they serve. It is important to get specific legal advice about insider relationships which may exist

Institutional Shareholders Pension funds, life insurance companies and other institutions that invest money on behalf of others

Letters Patent A document issued by the government granting the right to form a corporation (Prince Edward Island is the only jurisdiction in Canada that still forms corporations through the grant of letters patent)

Majority of the Minority A majority of the votes cast by disinterested shareholders

MD&A Management discussion and analysis of corporation's financial condition and results of operations issued with quarterly and annual financial reports

Memorandum of Association Basic charter document for forming a corporation in some provinces such as Nova Scotia

NACD National Association of Corporate Directors, a Washington-based organization focusing on board leadership issues (www.nacdonline.org)

OMERS Ontario Municipal Employees Retirement System, an institutional shareholder

OSC Ontario Securities Commission

OSC Rule 61-501 A rule under the *Securities Act* (Ontario) dealing with certain special transactions, such as issuer bids, insider bids, going private transactions and related party transactions. The provisions of Rule 61-501 deal with valuation, disclosure, minority approval and the independence of the board in the context of these transactions

Proxy A document signed by a shareholder authorizing another person to vote at a shareholders' meeting on behalf of the shareholder

Related Director A director who is not an unrelated director (defined below)

Reporting Issuer Public companies that are subject to securities regulator and securities law

Sarbanes-Oxley The *Sarbanes-Oxley Act of 2002*. Also referred to as "Sarbanes-Oxley" and "SarbOx". (U.S. legislation affecting companies with securities in the U.S.)

Saucier Report *Beyond Compliance: Building a Governance Culture*, Report of the Joint Committee on Corporate Governance released in November 2001. The committee was sponsored by the Canadian Institute of Chartered Accountants, the Canadian Venture Exchange and The Toronto Stock Exchange

SEC U.S. Securities and Exchange Commission

SEDAR System for Electronic Document Analysis and Retrieval, which has been used since January 1, 1997 to electronically file securities related information with the Canadian Securities Administrators. SEDAR can be accessed at www.sedar.com

Shareholder Agreement An agreement between some or all of the shareholders of a corporation relating to voting and transfer of shares and the corporation's business

TSX The Toronto Stock Exchange – Canada's national exchange for more senior issuers

TSX Guidelines 14 guidelines set out in the TSX Policy on Corporate Governance at section 474 of the TSX Company Manual

TSX Ventures TSX Ventures Exchange - Canada's national exchange for venture class securities

Unanimous Shareholders Agreement An agreement between all shareholders that restricts the powers of the board of directors as permitted by incorporation statutes. A Unanimous Shareholder Agreement forms part of the Charter Documents

Unrelated Director Under the TSX Guidelines, an "unrelated director" is a director who is independent of management and is free from any interest and any business or other relationship which could, or could reasonably be perceived to, materially interfere with the director's ability to act with a view to the best interests of the corporation, other than interests and relationships arising from shareholding

Index

misuse of corporate assets, 1
nominee directors, 111–114
outside ordinary course of business,
123–124, 133
professionalism, 49–50
removal by shareholders, 42
remuneration, 70–71
restriction of powers
by shareholders, 45–47
role in corporate governance,
generally, 1–2
stewardship function
generally, 2, 33
TSX Guidelines, 2–3
what directors need to know
(highlights), 28

DUTIES OF DIRECTORS
"business judgment rule", 13,
114–117
duty to creditors, 110
duty of care
applicable to all directors, 108
described, 106–107
due diligence
defined, 117–118
good faith requirement, 118
reliance
financial statements, 119
generally, 118
management, 118–119
outside advisors, 119–120
fiduciary duty
appropriation of corporate
opportunity, 102–104
Canaero decision, 109–110
confidentiality, 104
conflict of interest, 99, 100–102
defined, 98–99
disclosure, 104–105
irreconcilable differences, 106
generally, 97
stakeholders, to, 109, 110–111

ETHICAL TONE OF CORPORATION
setting by directors, 4

EXTERNAL AUDITOR See AUDITOR

GENERAL COUNSEL
role, 91–93

GLOSSARY, 185–189

GOVERNANCE AND NOMINATING
COMMITTEE
chair, 91
requirement to have (U.S), 85
TSX Guidelines, 38

ICD (INSTITUTE OF CORPORATE
DIRECTORS)
described, 117
director education, 19

INTERNAL AUDITOR
defined, 60
independence, 60
NYSE requirements, 61
reporting relationship, 60
role, 60

INVESTOR COMMUNITY
influence on governance issues, 36

LIABILITY OF DIRECTORS See also
PROTECTION OF DIRECTORS
FROM LIABILITY
authorizing corporation to commit
offence, 139–140
breach of duty to corporation,
150–151
dividends, declaring while insolvent,
140–142
due diligence defence, 117–120, 142
factors affecting, 138

Special Inserts

The following is an index to the special inserts that appear throughout this book.

APPENDIX

2002 / 2003 in Review

U.S. Corporate Governance Developments

TOP GOVERNANCE STORIES IN 2002 / 2003

It is difficult to imagine that there will be another year with as many stories focusing on failures of governance as there were in 2002. Highlights of some of the top stories in the United States are set out below.

ENRON CORP. slid into bankruptcy in the fall of 2001, and continued to be the top corporate governance story throughout 2002. In February, the report of the special investigative committee of the Enron board (referred to as the "Powers Report") described a number of improper financial transactions and extensive self-dealing by company officers. It concluded that Enron's board and audit committee had failed in the discharge of their responsibilities.

. Congressional hearings into Enron's collapse were held throughout 2002. Kenneth Lay (Enron's former chair), Andrew Fastow (Enron's former CFO) and other former Enron executives refused to testify at those hearings, invoking their Fifth Amendment rights against self-incrimination. Jeffrey Skilling, Enron's former CEO, appeared, only to testify that he was not aware of any wrong-doing at Enron. In July, a subcommittee of the U.S. Senate released a report entitled "The Role of the Board of Directors in Enron's Collapse", finding that the board had contributed to Enron's demise.

In August 2002, former Enron executive Michael Kopper pleaded guilty to money laundering and conspiracy to commit wire fraud and named Andrew Fastow as an unindicted co-conspirator. Fastow was later indicted on 78 counts of federal fraud, conspiracy and money laundering.

Arthur Andersen, Enron's former auditor, did not survive its involvement with Enron. Serious concern have been raised in many quarters about Andersen's relationship with Enron, the quality of its audit and the role that these factors may have played in Enron's downfall. These issues are just beginning to make their way through the legal system. However, it was not these issues, but rather the actions of certain Andersen partners and employees after Enron filed for bankruptcy that brought Andersen down. In June 2002, Andersen was found guilty of obstructing an investigation into Enron and within months had surrendered its licences to practise accounting in every U.S. state. Portions of its practice were acquired by other accounting firms and most of the remaining professionals and staff were forced to seek other employment. Andersen partners lost their jobs, positions, careers and the capital they had invested in the firm and are continuing to live with the prospect of additional liability.

Investigations into the conduct of various Enron executives continues throughout 2003. In May 2003, the SEC filed a complaint against several former executives of Enron Broadband Services, Enron's high-speed telecommunications unit. The SEC alleges that the executives misled investors in their descriptions of the division's performance and prospects.

In May 2003, the plethora of actions involving Enron led federal judges overseeing Enron's bankruptcy and certain lawsuits relating to the bankruptcy to order a mediation aimed at settling the various actions.

ADELPHIA CORP. announced in May that it had launched a probe into allegations of improper use of hundreds of millions of dollars in corporate funds by its founder John Rigas and members of his family. Rigas resigned his position as CEO at the request of the independent members of the board and his sons resigned their executive positions a short time later. All three members of the Rigas family, together with two other former Adelphia executives, have been indicted on fraud charges. The SEC has filed civil charges against Adelphia and its former executives and Adelphia has sued the Rigases. Adelphia's board removed its auditors in June, blaming them for not informing them about questionable accounting and self-dealing at the cable company. Adelphia filed for bankruptcy protection in June 2002.

GENERAL ELECTRIC and its former chairman Jack Welch came under fire when the benefits and perquisites that Mr. Welch was receiving following his retirement from GE became public in September 2002. Divorce papers filed against Mr. Welch described his use of a Manhattan apartment and aircraft owned by GE as well as corporate aircraft, tickets to various sporting events and expensive dinners paid for by the company. The retirement contract between GE and Mr. Welch was ultimately modified, leaving Mr. Welch only with office and administrative support.

GLOBAL CROSSING filed for bankruptcy protection in January 2002, becoming the fourth largest bankruptcy in U.S. history. It has been accused of engaging in misleading accounting methods to report millions of dollars in sales and cash revenues that did not exist.

IMCLONE SYSTEMS INC. was advised in January 2002, that the U.S. Federal Drug Administration had rejected its application to market the cancer drug, Erbitux. In May, CEO Sam Waksal resigned and in August he was indicted on charges resulting from allegations that he had tried to sell shares in ImClone before news of the FDA decision had been released and had tipped friends and family (including Martha Stewart) to the information in advance. In October he pleaded guilty to a number of these charges, including insider trading. In September, a Merrill Lynch brokerage assistant pleaded guilty to a misdemeanour charge and provided testimony to federal prosecutors against Martha Stewart and others.

In June 2003, Ms. Stewart was indicted on five criminal counts of securities fraud, conspiracy and making false statements to federal agents. Her former stockbroker at Merrill Lynch, Peter Bacanovic, was also indicted. In a separate civil case, the SEC has accused Ms. Stewart of insider trading. Several days before Ms. Stewart's indictment, Mr. Waksal was sentenced to seven years and three months in prison for insider trading, obstructing justice and tax evasion, the harshest sentence possible.

KMART CORP. filed for bankruptcy in January 2002. In early 2003, a stewardship review prepared by Kmart's bankruptcy counsel and two forensic accounting firms was released. Among other things, it found that Kmart's financial statements had been manipulated by senior management during the first three quarters of 2001 (including $92 million in questionable vendor transactions), that former Kmart executives had altered information submitted to Kmart's board of directors about a $24 million loan program for key executives and that former management had spent $12 million on aircraft without proper budget authorization. In February 2003, the SEC charged two former Kmart executives with accounting fraud.

Kmart emerged from bankruptcy in April 2003.

SALOMON SMITH BARNEY was among the investment banks being investigated by New York State Attorney General Eliot Spitzer in 2002. The relationships of analyst Jack Grubman to the issuers he covered have been of particular interest. Mr. Grubman resigned in August 2002, following widespread criticism of his stock recommendations and allegations that he had misled investors. Among the criticisms of Mr. Grubman are his close relationship with executives of WorldCom, a company which he consistently rated highly, ultimately downgrading it to "neutral" only after it had lost 90% of its value. E-mails from Mr. Grubman obtained by the Wall Street Journal led to allegations that he had upgraded his rating of AT&T stock in return for a $1 million donation which his employer made to an exclusive nursery school where Mr. Grubman subsequently enrolled his children.

In April 2003, 10 of the largest securities firms in the United States (including Salomon Smith Barney) agreed to pay $1.4 billon to settle charges by the SEC and other securities regulators that the firms had routinely issued overly optimistic stock research to further the interests of clients from whom they earned significant investment banking fees. The penalties also included lifetime bans from the securities industry for Mr. Grubman and Henry Blodget of Merrill Lynch & Co. Mr. Grubman and Mr. Blodget were charged with issuing fraudulent research reports and agreed to pay penalties of $15 million and $4 million, respectively.

TYCO CEO Dennis Kozlowski resigned amid rumours that he was about to be charged with tax evasion (charges that were ultimately laid). Tyco has launched several suits against Kozlowski, several other employees and its former lead director for, among other things, having unauthorized payments and other exercises in self-dealing in amounts estimated to have totalled $600 million.

In June 2002, Kozlowski and former CFO Mark Swartz were charged by New York prosecutors with grand larceny, enterprise corruption and falsifying business records in connection with their alleged theft of more than $170 million from Tyco. Prosecutors have accused them of running a "criminal enterprise" aimed at defrauding investors. The general counsel was also criminally charged.

The state of play at Tyco remains unsettled. A report by the law firm of Boies, Schiller & Flexner LLP in September 2002 concluded that there had been a pattern of "aggressive accounting", but that there hadn't been any systemic or significant fraud relating to the company's financial statements. However, throughout 2003, Tyco has announced a series of further accounting charges necessary to clean up its books, bringing the reliability of the Boies report into question. The SEC and the Manhattan district attorney's office are continuing with their investigations of Tyco's accounting practices.

WORLDCOM (now MCI) CEO Bernard Ebbers revealed in January 2002 that he owed WorldCom $339.7 million in loans he took out to buy shares in the telecommunications giant. A short time later, WorldCom announced that its 2001 fourth-quarter income was down by 64% and that it expected a second-quarter charge of $15-$20 billion to write down the value of some acquired assets. In April, after WorldCom had once again announced a dramatic drop in earnings (a 78% decline in first-quarter net income), Ebbers resigned. Several months later, it announced that $3.8 billion in expenses had been improperly booked as capital expenditures. By August this number had grown to $7.2 billion and by November to $9 billion. WorldCom filed for bankruptcy protection in July—the largest bankruptcy filing in U.S. history.

The SEC's action against WorldCom alleged that it had engaged in "massive accounting fraud." That action was settled in late November 2002. Former CFO Scott Sullivan, together with a mid-level accounting executive said to have carried out Mr. Sullivan's orders, have been indicted on a number of charges, including securities fraud. WorldCom's ex-controller, David Myers, pleaded guilty to fraud, saying that he was instructed by senior management to make entries each quarter to falsify WorldCom's books to reduce its reported actual costs. Admissions of guilt from other former World-Com executives followed.

In November 2002, New York State Attorney General Eliot Spitzer sued former WorldCom CEO Bernard Ebbers and four other executives with profiting improperly from IPO offerings given to them by Salomon Smith Barney to secure WorldCom's investment banking business.

On June 10, 2003, two separate reports were released which concluded that Mr. Ebbers, other members of management and a long list of employees had conspired to carry out massive and systematic fraud at WorldCom. One was a report of William McLucas at Wilmer, Butler & Pickering LLP, counsel to the special committee of MCI's board of directors. In releasing the report, the board stated that it had commissioned the report to ensure that everyone knows exactly what transpired in the past and that new controls would be implemented so that history would not repeat itself. The other report was the Second Interim Report of the Examiner in the WorldCom bankruptcy. The Examiner noted that "... [w]hile the degree of responsibility varies greatly, WorldCom could not have failed as a result of the actions of a limited number of individuals. Rather, there was a broad breakdown of the system of internal controls, corporate governance and individual responsibility, all of which worked together to create a culture in which few persons took responsibility until it was too late."

XEROX CORP. agreed in April 2002 to restate its earnings for four years and pay a $10 million civil penalty to settle SEC charges that it engaged in fraudulent accounting practices — the largest penalty ever levied against a public company in connection with financial reporting violations. A new audit of Xerox's financial statements revealed even bigger accounting issues — Xerox announced that there could be as much as $6 billion of improperly recorded revenue over a five-year period — twice what the SEC had estimated when it reached its settlement with Xerox.

In January 2003 the SEC charged Xerox's auditors (and four partners of that firm) with fraud, alleging that they permitted Xerox to manipulate its accounting practices to close a $3 million gap between actual reporting results and the results reported to the public.

On June 5, 2003, the SEC announced that six former Xerox executives agreed to pay $22 million in fines and other penalties to settle civil fraud charges brought against them by the SEC. The amounts to be paid include significant civil penalties ($1 million each in the case of former CEO Paul Allaire and former CFO Barry Romeril) as well as disgorgement of incentives paid to them by Xerox and gains made by the executives in selling their shares of Xerox. The SEC also imposed a bar on three of the executives from serving as a director or officer of a public company. Xerox has stated that its by-laws obliged it to indemnify the executives for their legal fees and the amounts they were required to disgorge (but not the civil penalties).

The complaint against the former executives alleged in part that:

- Mr. Allaire and Mr. Romeril, together with Richard Thoman, the former President and COO, set a "tone at the top" at Xerox which equated business success with meeting short-term earnings targets;

- Mr. Romeril directed or allowed lower ranking defendants in Xerox's financial department to make accounting adjustments to results reported from operating divisions to accelerate revenues and increase earnings;

- Philip Fishbach (former Controller), Daniel Marchibroda (former assistant Controller) and Gregory Tayler (former Director of Accounting Policy) adopted and applied the accounting devices for the purpose of meeting earnings goals and predictions of outside securities analysts;

- Mr. Allaire and Mr. Thoman then announced these results to the public through meetings with analysts and in communications to shareholders, celebrating that Xerox was enjoying substantially greater earnings growth than true operating results warranted.

The U.S. Department of Justice continues to pursue its criminal investigation against Xerox's former executives.

LEGISLATIVE AND REGULATORY DEVELOPMENTS IN 2002 / 2003

The *Sarbanes-Oxley Act of 2002* was enacted on July 30, 2002. It is referred to variously as "Sarbanes-Oxley", "SarbOx" and "SOX" and represents an extensive legislative intervention into the governance of public companies. Many of the provisions of Sarbanes-Oxley did not come into effect immediately, because it was necessary for the SEC to develop and enact implementary rules to give effect to those provisions. The SEC is currently in the process of proposing and finalizing those rules. The following is an overview of the areas addressed in Sarbanes-Oxley:

- Audit committees (additional independence requirements for audit committee members; disclosure of whether there is a financial expert on the audit committee; enhanced audit committee responsibility for oversight of the audit function; procedures for receiving and handling complaints; and authority to engage advisors).
- Senior officers (certification of reports; code of ethics for senior financial officers; ban on loans to management; forfeiture by CEO and CFO of certain bonuses and profits; sanctions for improper influence on the conduct of audits; prohibition on insider trades during pension fund blackout periods; director and officer bans and penalties; and accelerated insider trading filing).
- Auditors (new independence requirements; mandatory partner rotation; reports to the audit committee; new regulatory process; and new restrictions on non-audit services).

- Disclosure requirements (audit committee mandate; whether the audit committee has a financial expert; assessments by independent auditor of internal controls, disclosure of off-balance sheet financing and financial contingencies; real time disclosure, enhanced SEC powers with respect to disclosure; regulation of pro forma financial information; and financial reports filed with SEC must report all material correction adjustments identified by auditor).
- Other (analyst conflicts of interest; rules of professional responsibility for attorneys; whistle blower protection; debts non-dischargeable in bankruptcy; temporary freeze authority for SEC; and SEC censure).

Prior to the enactment of Sarbanes-Oxley, both the NYSE and Nasdaq proposed extensive amendments to their corporate governance listing requirements. These proposals were revised in early August to take the provisions of Sarbanes-Oxley into account and certain further amendments to the proposed definition of independence were released in April 2003. The revised amendments are still being reviewed by the SEC. The following is an overview of the areas addressed in the proposed amendments to the NYSE requirements:

- Board issues (tighter standards for director independence (not applicable to controlled corporations); requirement for regular *in camera* meetings; and requirement for nominating/corporate governance committee and compensation committee, each composed entirely of independent directors [not applicable to controlled companies]).
- Audit committees (disallowed compensation for audit committee members; written mandate addressing certain matters; and responsibilities for the appointments, compensation and oversight of the external auditor, including approving all non-audit engagements).
- Other (internal audit function required; shareholder approval of equity-compensation plans; corporate governance guidelines; code of business conduct; CEO certification of compliance; and letter of reprimand).

Canadian Corporate Governance Developments

TOP GOVERNANCE STORIES IN 2002 / 2003

Failures in corporate governance have been linked to corporate performance in Canada as well as in the United States. The following is a summary of the top governance stories, in 2002 and the first half of 2003.

BRE-X MINERALS LTD. was a Calgary-based public mining company with a market value at its height of $4.5 billion. In 1997, it was revealed that there was no gold at its mine in Busang. Samples of mined rock from that site were shown to have been salted with gold flakes from another location. Bre-X subsequently filed for bankruptcy.

The Royal Canadian Mounted Police were not able to amass sufficient evidence to bring criminal charges against Bre-X, its officers or directors. The Ontario Securities Commission took action against John B. Felderhof, Bre-X's top geologist and vice chairman, charging him with insider trading and misleading investors. That action continued to be stalled by procedural arguments before the court throughout 2002. Various class actions involving Bre-X also moved forward in both the United States and Canada, some ultimately being resolved in settlement.

CINAR CORP., a producer of children's programming, has been embroiled in financial scandals involving its founders Micheline Charest and Ronald Weinberg. Allegations include improper use of tax credits (on the basis that certain American scripts were represented to have been written by Canadians), fraudulent script royalties paid to Ms. Charest's sister, unauthorized offshore investments of over US$120 million and improper use of corporate assets by Ms. Charest, Mr. Weinberg and another Cinar executive.

In 2002, the Quebec Securities Commission fined Ms. Charest and Mr. Weinberg $1 million each and banned them from exercising their controlling shares of Cinar or acting as directors or executives of any Canadian public company for five years, the stiffest penalties ever imposed by the QSC. Cinar has settled certain of the law suits against it, including class action suits brought by shareholders. Other actions remain ongoing.

HYDRO ONE is the government owned electricity transmission utility in the Province of Ontario. Plans to privatize Hydro One announced late in 2001 hit a number of legal obstacles in 2002, which ultimately led opposition parties and the press to focus on the compensation packages of senior executives at Hydro One. Those packages included generous termination arrangements. The government ordered Hydro One's board to review the compensation packages. Dissatisfied with the board's proposal to reduce remuneration and benefits for the Hydro One executives, the government introduced legislation to fire the board and roll back salary and severance entitlements. The directors resigned *en masse* and a new board was appointed. One of the first actions of the new board was to fire CEO Eleanor Clitheroe. Board chair, Glen Wright, alleged publicly that Ms. Clitheroe had misused corporate assets. Ms. Clitheroe countered that all amounts received had been approved by the previous board chairman, Sir Graham Day. She commenced a $31 million lawsuit against Hydro One, alleging slander among other things.

LIVENT INC. was founded by Garth Drabinsky and Myron Gottlieb in 1990 and became one of North America's leading theatre companies. In 1998, Hollywood agent Michael Ovitz and New York investment banker Roy Furman acquired control of Livent and several months later made accusations of accounting irregularities. Law suits were launched by both sides. Livent subsequently lapsed into bankruptcy.

In January 1999, Mr. Drabinsky and Mr. Gottlieb were charged in the United States with criminal fraud and conspiracy in connection with alleged accounting irregularities. A warrant was issued for their arrest when they failed to appear in U.S. federal court to hear the charges. They also face a variety of SEC charges. Two other former Livent executives pleaded guilty to U.S. criminal charges relating to the alleged fraud.

In July 2001, the OSC accused Mr. Drabinsky, Mr. Gottlieb and two other former Livent executives with taking a variety of actions contrary to the public interest, including filing misleading financial statements. In October 2002, the RCMP laid charges against Mr. Drabinsky, Mr. Gottlieb and two other former Livent executives, saying that they had perpetrated a "massive fraud against the Canadian public" by falsifying Livent's financial statements and thereby misrepresenting its financial health.

YBM MAGNEX INTERNATIONAL INC. presented itself as being in the business of manufacturing and selling industrial magnets. Whether or the extent to which it was in fact engaged in this business is the subject of ongoing investigation and litigation. In Canada, the OSC has been hearing arguments relating to allegations that YBM, its directors and underwriters failed in their obligation to provide full, true and plain disclosure in a prospectus issued by YBM in 1997.

YBM was incorporated in 1994 as Pratecs Technologies Inc., a junior capital pool company with shares listed on the Alberta Stock Exchange. It merged with a Pennsylvania company in 1995 and listed its shares on the TSX the following year.

In March 1996, the board of directors of YBM was advised by its outside counsel that the company was the target of a U.S. federal investigation, although it was not clear why. The board formed a special committee which retained various advisors and became aware of allegations that YBM was connected to an organized crime syndicate in Russia and that its financial records and customer lists may have been falsified. The extent to which the various (and often conflicting) reports from various experts and advisors justified a conclusion by the board that these allegations were without substance is the subject of ongoing investigation.

In November 1997, YBM went to the capital markets and raised $53 million under a prospectus and another $48 million in a private placement. The disclosure in connection with the prospectus offering gave rise to the action by the OSC referred to above.

Six months after the public offering (In May 1998), the YBM offices in Pennsylvania were raided by a number of U.S. authorities including the FBI, the IRS and U.S. Immigration. A month later, forensic auditors confirmed that YBM's customer list had been fabricated. YBM went into bankruptcy in December 1998. The receiver later pleaded guilty to charges of fraud and paid a $3 million fine.

Two class actions against YBM were settled and approved by the

Ontario Superior Court in May 2002. The OSC took action against YBM, its directors and officers, as well as its underwriters. An overview of that decision can be found at the end of this section under "June 2003 Update".

CHRONOLOGY OF CANADIAN LEGISLATIVE AND REGULATORY DEVELOPMENTS IN 2002 / 2003

In November 2001, the Joint Committee on Corporate Governance (known as the "Saucier Committee" for its chair, Guylaine Saucier) released its report, *Beyond Compliance: Building a Governance Culture*. Among other things, the Saucier Report recommended certain changes to the TSX's corporate governance guidelines and the introduction of a new condition of continued listing that would require the board of every TSX listed company to have an "independent board leader" who would perform certain functions described in the Saucier Report in greater detail.

In April 2002, the TSX released proposed amendments to its corporate governance guidelines, accepting some, but not all, of the recommendations in the Saucier Report. When Sarbanes-Oxley was enacted in the United States, the TSX put these proposals on hold. In November 2002, it proposed revised, much harder hitting amendments to both its listing requirements and its corporate governance guidelines. The revised proposals have been submitted to the OSC for approval. It is expected that these proposals (incorporating whatever further changes may be added in the interim) will be published for public comment before they are finalized and implemented.

In early August 2002, the OSC's continuous disclosure team commenced a special review of the disclosure of Ontario's 44 largest reporting issuers. As part of this review, it requested certain corporate records of these issuers, including materials provided to the audit committee and minutes of meetings of the audit committees of these reporting issuers. Although the issuers were generally highly responsive to the OSC's request for these records, concern was expressed by members of the legal and accounting professions about the confidentiality of these materials and the chill on disclosure to and discussions with the audit committee that could result if these records were routinely requested by securities regulators.

In response to developments in the United States, including the enactment of Sarbanes-Oxley, OSC Chair David Brown commenced a consultation process with the TSX and with capital market participants. On August 15, 2002 he sent an open letter to Barbara Stymiest, Chief Executive Officer of the TSX Group, asking for the TSX's views on:

- whether it would be appropriate to adopt similar measures in Canada;
- whether these measures should be mandatory; and
- whether some or all of the TSX corporate governance guidelines, and additional guidelines recommended by the Saucier Committee, should become mandatory requirements.

Ms. Stymiest responded on September 17, 2002, saying that, for the most part, the TSX should continue its tradition of voluntary compliance with principles set out in corporate governance guidelines. She recommended that TSX listed companies be required to have at least two unrelated directors and an audit committee with a written charter. She recommended certain changes to the TSX Guidelines, but that they remain voluntary, disclosure-based guidelines. Concurrently, Linda Hohol, President of the TSX Ventures Exchange, wrote to Stephen Sibold (Chair of the Alberta Securities Commission) and Douglas Hyndman (Chair of the British Columbia Securities Commission) on behalf of the TSX Ventures Exchange, noting that enhanced corporate governance requirements would be prohibitively expensive for many TSX Ventures listed companies. She also argued that they are largely unnecessary, since the TSX Ventures Exchange performs a much greater oversight function with respect to an issuer's corporate structure and transaction terms than is necessary for the TSX to do.

On October 30, 2002 the Ontario government introduced Bill 198 which, among other things, proposed certain corporate governance-related amendments to the *Securities Act*. Bill 198 passed into law on December 9, 2002 but only certain provisions amending the *Securities Act* have not yet been proclaimed into force. The amendments that came into force in early April 2003, have given the OSC the remaining rule-making authority necessary to allow it to require CEOs and CFOs to certify their company's financial statements, just as they are required to do in the United States under Sarbanes-Oxley. In addition, the OSC has the authority to make rules with respect to audit committees. As expected, the OSC has used this new authority to require all reporting issuers to have audit committees (audit committees are currently requirements under corporate law) and to impose certain requirements with respect to the composition and mandate of audit committees (for details see "June 2003 Update"). The amendments also specifically recognize the role of the continuous disclosure review team at the OSC and empower it to require issuers to deliver to it documents that are relevant to the disclosure made or that ought to have been made. These and many of the other amendments to the *Securities Act* in Bill 198 were adopted from the recommendations of the draft report of the Five Year Review Committee tabled in May 2002.

The amendments to the *Securities Act* introduced under Bill 198 that have not been proclaimed into force include those that will introduce statutory civil liability for secondary market disclosure. This will give investors a statutory basis on which to sue the issuer, its directors and officers, among others, for misrepresentations in the issuer's public disclosures and for failure to make timely disclosures. These amendments are undergoing certain technical refinements but are expected to come into force later this year.

On October 31, 2002, OSC Chair David Brown issued a progress report to capital market participants on the action being taken by the OSC to restore investor confidence. The letter setting out this progress report read in part as follows:

> *Let me reiterate the importance of addressing this issue. Clearly, there has been a spillover effect in Canada from the damage to investor confidence in the U.S. We cannot ignore the regulatory overhaul in the world's largest economy, which is so tightly interwoven with our own. As the regulator of Canada's largest capital market, we must take steps to respond to these changes.*

The amendments being proposed by the TSX include the introduction of certain conditions to listing as well as amendments to the TSX Guidelines. The proposed amendments are currently being reviewed by the OSC. The final form of the proposals will be published for a public comment period. Once they are finalized, it is expected that there will be a transition period before the amendments come into effect.

The Proposed TSX Amendments would introduce the following conditions to continued listing:

Audit Committee Requirements

- Every listed company must have an audit committee composed of a majority of unrelated directors.
- The board must adopt a formal charter for the audit committee.
- The audit committee charter must be published in the issuer's annual report or information circular once every three years or following a material amendment to the charter.

Board Composition

- The board of every listed issuer must include at least two "unrelated directors" at all times (note that the definition of "unrelated director" will also be amended).

Formal Code of Business Ethics or Business Conduct

- The board of every listed issuer must adopt a formal code of business ethics or business conduct that governs the behaviour of its directors, officers and employees.
- The code must be published in the annual report or information circular once every three years or following any material amendment.
- The board must monitor compliance with the code.
- The board must be responsible for granting any waivers from compliance for directors and officers and must disclose such waivers in the next quarterly report (with the circumstances and rationale for granting the waiver).

In addition to the amendment to the definition of "unrelated director" discussed above, the Proposed TSX Amendments would introduce certain other amendments to the TSX Guidelines, the most significant of which would recommend that:

- The compensation committee and audit committee must both be composed of unrelated directors (which is a higher standard than the listing requirement described above for the audit committee which requires only a majority of unrelated directors).
- The compensation committee must be composed solely of unrelated directors.
- Other committees must generally be composed solely of non-management directors, a majority of whom are unrelated directors.
- All members of the audit committee be financially literate and at least one member have accounting or related financial experience.
- The audit committee must have oversight of internal control.
- The audit committee charter must include certain specified responsibilities.

The Proposed TSX Amendments would also introduce Practice Notes to assist in the interpretation of the guidelines, provide that the TSX will review the governance disclosure of listed companies on a selected basis each year and allow for the TSX to make certain exemptions in respect of its corporate governance policy.

As this book went to press, the OSC was about to release its new rules relating to CEO/CFO certification and audit committees. These proposed rules will be open for a 90-day comment period and are expected to come in force before the end of 2003. For more details see "June 2003 Update" at the end of this section.

RULES VS. PRINCIPLES: THE CANADIAN DEBATE

The Canadian business community watched corporate developments in the United States closely throughout 2002. The discussion about how Canadian corporations and regulators should proceed polarized into a debate about the rules versus principles approach to corporate governance: whether the global nature of capital markets made it desirable (if not necessary) for Canadian regulators to follow the American approach or whether a made in Canada solution could be found. In her response to David's Brown's letter, Barbara Stymiest, Chief Executive Officer of the TSX, described the differences between the Canadian and the U.S. approach:

...our Canadian approach has been to set out comprehensive governance guidelines based on the paramountcy of the underlying principles that are involved. We then require that companies disclose the extent of their compliance with the guidelines and explain publicly why they may choose not to follow certain of them. In the U.K., European and Australian markets, a similar principles-based approach is preferred.

The effect of strong guidelines in combination with mandatory disclosure is to place in the hands of investors the information they require to punish or reward companies, by their trading and pricing choices, for their governance practices.

The American approach, in contrast, has been heavily oriented toward mandatory compliance with highly detailed legislation, regulation and stock exchange listing requirements, with a much greater emphasis on regulatory enforcement rather than voluntary compliance.

In his remarks to the Senate Committee on Banking, Trade & Commerce on October 30, 2002, David Brown set out the argument for more regulation of corporate governance practices:

To the extent that a change in attitude can solve a problem, we are already seeing considerable progress. We are seeing large companies voluntarily committing to improve their forms of corporate governance and enhancing voluntary disclosure. A coalition of senior executives has adopted a new voluntary code for its members. And we are seeing large investors making improved governance and transparency a priority and promising to hold corporations to their commitments.

This market self-correction is an important step forward. But there is a limit to a market's ability to correct itself, especially in areas like audit quality, disclosure standards and conflict of interest. As we have seen, corporate executives don't always have the right incentives to follow the appropriate practices. Investors don't necessarily have all of the information needed to police them.

We are not content to see some corporations improve their practices while others lag significantly behind. We have to lock those practices in—and make them a market norm.

By strengthening and clarifying requirements in financial reporting and corporate governance — as opposed to simply encouraging voluntary action — we can ensure that high standards are followed consistently by all public companies. We can level the playing field and ensure consistent corporate behaviour. Thus, high standards of transparency and accountability become the floor that all traded companies stand on, rather than a ceiling that many never approach.

By locking in reform, we can ensure that it does not follow the cyclical pattern that characterizes so many market corrections: they tend to be born in down markets but lost to the irrational exuberance of boom markets.

Locking in reform also ensures that standards are comparable across the country. Otherwise some companies may be tempted to pursue a competitive search for the weakest regulatory regimes, prompting a race to the bottom. In that respect, the OSC is pleased to be working closely with our colleagues in the other 12 provincial and territorial commissions.

The integrity of our capital markets is too important to be left entirely to voluntary action. Today, people can invest wherever they want. We have to give them the confidence they need to invest here.

It comes down to this: Public confidence in financial reporting and corporate governance cannot depend on individual commitment and judgment. It must be backed up by regulation.

In its report, Navigating Through "The Perfect Storm": Safeguards to Restore Investor Confidence, the Senate Committee on Banking, Trade and Commerce agreed with Mr. Brown that it is necessary to "lock in" reforms in financial reporting and corporate governance through legislation. The report reads in part as follows:

Simply importing the Sarbanes-Oxley Act of 2002 into Canada would not be appropriate, since doing so would not recognize the strengths and initiatives that currently exist and might not be appropriate to our needs. On the other hand, continuing with a non-legislative approach, and perpetuating mandatory disclosure, voluntary compliance, rules and policies is also not appropriate in our view, since we believe that enhanced investor confidence in Canada requires certain legislative proposals, as was the case in the United States.

JUNE 2003 UPDATE

There were a number of developments in corporate governance in Canada as this book was going to print in June 2003. These developments are summarized below.

PROPOSED AMENDMENTS TO THE CRIMINAL CODE

On June 12, 2003 the federal government introduced Bill C-46, dealing with capital markets fraud and Bill C-45, dealing with criminal liability of organizations. Highlights of each of these bills is set out below.

Bill C-46 (Capital Markets Fraud)

Bill C-46 creates new indictable offences for insider trading. Both the concept of "insider" and of "inside information" are cast differently than they are in provincial securities legislation. However, unlike provincial securities laws, the Crown must prove that the insider knowingly used the inside information in trading in the security. The offence would carry a possible penalty of up to 10 years in prison.

Bill C-46 also creates a new indictable offence for tipping. The concept of "tipping" in Bill C-46 means knowingly conveying inside information relevant to a security to another person, knowing that that person might use that information in trading in a security. Punishment is up to five years in prison.

Bill C-46 also creates a new indictable offence for employers who take certain actions against their employees intended to prevent the employee from providing certain information to law enforcement authorities or retaliating against the employee for having done so. The offence would carry a possible penalty of up to 10 years in prison.

Finally, Bill C-46 would increase the penalties for defrauding the public or any person of property, money or valuable securities and for engaging in intentionally fraudulent acts that affect the public market price of shares to a maximum of 14 years (it is currently 10 years).

Bill C-45 (Criminal Liability of an Organization)

Whether a corporation can be held liable for the criminal activities of its directors, officers and employees is currently a matter of common law in Canada. In other words, this liability is based on principles developed by the courts, not by legislators. Bill C-45 would introduce a new statutory regime for attributing criminal liability to corporations and other organizations in some cases.

Bill C-45 provides that, if a director, officer, employee, agent or contractor of an organization commits the offence of criminal negligence, the organization may also be liable if the actions of the senior officer of the organization who was responsible for those activities departed markedly from the standard of care that could reasonably have been expected to prevent that person's involvement in the offence. In addition, the organization may be deemed to be a party to an intentional criminal offence committed by one of its representatives if a senior officer was knowingly involved in the offence or was aware of the offence and knowingly failed to take all reasonable measures to stop the representative's participation in the offence.

Bill C-45 also imposes a duty on every person who undertakes, or has the authority to direct how a person does work or performs a task, to take reasonable steps to prevent bodily harm to the person or any other person arising from that work or task.

It should also be noted that Bill C-45 will introduce new sentencing guidelines for capital markets offences. In handing down a sentence with respect to a capital markets offence, the courts will be required to consider a new set of "aggravating circumstances". These "aggravating circumstances" include a fraud of over $1 million, the potential or actual adverse effect of the offence on the stability of the Canadian economy, financial system or market in Canada or investor confidence; the involvement of a large number of victims; and whether the offender took advantage of the high regard in which the offender was held in the community in committing the offence. The courts will be required to disregard the offender's employment, skills and status in the community as mitigating factors if those circumstances were relevant to, or were used in the commission of the offence.

REPORT OF THE SENATE BANKING COMMITTEE

In June 2003, the Standing Senate Committee on Banking, Trade and Commerce released its report entitled *Navigating Through "The Perfect Storm": Safeguards to Restore Investor Confidence* (referred to here as the "Senate Committee Report"). The report was the result of the work of the Committee commencing in May 2002 in response to Enron and other corporate scandals in the United States. The Committee studied the circumstances which gave rise to these scandals in the United States with a particular focus on whether these circumstances could occur in Canada (with similar results) and, if so, how they might be avoided. The Senate Committee recommended legislation to mandate the following:

Board of Directors

- majority of the board must be independent (recognizing the special circumstances of closely held corporations and small and medium-sized businesses)
- independent directors must meet *in camera* on a periodic basis
- development of a code of directors to be followed by all members of the board

Audit Committee

- all members of audit committees must be independent and financially literate and at least one member should be a financial expert
- audit committee must have the ability to select and take advice from an independent audit advisor
- audit committee must meet *in camera* with the auditor
- audit committee must oversee the auditor selected by the shareholders

Auditor

- limits on non-audit services that auditors can provide to their audit clients (with possible exceptions for small and medium-sized businesses)
- rotation of the lead audit partner every seven consecutive years

Compensation Committee

- management may not sit on the compensation committee
- members of the compensation committee must have a level of expertise in the areas of compensation and human resource management

- compensation committee must be able to select and take advice from an independent compensation consultant
- compensation committee must meet in camera with the company's compensation consultant

Financial Analysts
- obviate real or perceived conflicts of interest by financial analysts

Whistleblowing
- whistleblower protection for employees with respect to the reporting of financial irregularities and failed corporate governance

Separation of CEO and Chair
- separation of the positions of CEO and Chair (bearing in mind the special circumstances that may exist with closely held companies and small and medium-sized businesses)

Certification of Financial Statements
- CEO and CFO to certify that the annual financial statements fairly present, in all material respects, both the results of the organization's operations and its financial condition

The Senate Report also recommends:
- provincial/territorial and private sector support for director education
- review of legislation to ensure that the accounting profession benefits from modified proportionate (rather than joint and several) liability
- review of legislation dealing with fraud, insider trading (including the adequacy of procedures and resources to ensure that corporate corruption is being prosecuted) with a view to implementing any changes needed as soon as possible
- federal government should work with appropriate organizations toward the development of global uniform accounting standards

YBM DECISION

On June 24, 2003, the Ontario Securities Commission released its decision in YBM Magnex International Inc. YBM was a TSX listed company that presented itself as being in the business of manufacturing and selling industrial magnets. The decision dealt with whether

YBM, its directors and underwriters failed in their obligation to provide full, true and plain disclosure in a prospectus issued by YBM in 1997.

In August 1996, the board of directors of YBM was advised by its outside counsel that the company was the target of a U.S. federal investigation, although it was not clear why. The board formed a special committee which retained various advisors and became aware of allegations that YBM was connected to an organized crime syndicate in Russia and that its financial records and customer lists may have been falsified. When it went to the capital markets the following year, it did not disclose in the prospectus what the OSC referred to as "unique risks": The decisions states that "[a]t a minimum, we believe some disclosure regarding what YBM knew about the U.S. investigation and less muddled disclosure regarding the purpose of the Special Committee would have better informed investors about the risks facing YBM". The OSC found YBM's disclosure to be materially misleading.

OSC Decision on Each of the Directors

Of the eight members of YBM's board of directors, five were sanctioned:

- Jacob Bogatin (YBM's CEO) and Igor Fisherman (YBM's COO) have been permanently prohibited from becoming or acting as a director or officer of any issuer.
- Owen Mitchell (Chair of the Special Committee and a Vice President of First Marathon, one of YBM's underwriters) was required to resign any positions he held as a director or officer of a reporting issuer and is prohibited from acting as a director or officer of any reporting issuer for five years. He was also required to pay investigation and hearing costs in the amount of $250,000.
- Keith Davies (member of the Special Committee) was required to resign any positions he held as a director or officer of a reporting issuer and is prohibited from acting as a director or officer of any reporting issuer for three years. He was also required to pay investigation and hearing costs in the amount of $75,000.
- Harry Antes (Chair of the YBM board and member of the Special Committee) was required to resign any positions he held

as a director or officer of a reporting issuer and is prohibited from acting as a director or officer of any reporting issuer for three years. He was also required to pay investigation and hearing costs in the amount of $75,000.

The remaining three directors were not sanctioned:

- David Peterson was Chair of the law firm of Cassels Brock (YBM's outside counsel) and a former Premier of Ontario. He was not a member of the Special Committee. The OSC found that a due diligence defence was available to him, but "just barely" and expressed disappointment that he had not offered more insight and leadership to the board in the circumstances.
- Frank Greenwald was (like Harry Antes) a retired scientist living in the United States and had been asked to join the YBM board because of his scientific expertise, experience, connections and standing within the magnetics industry. He was the chair of the Audit Committee, but was not on the Special Committee. The OSC found that he was not involved in and did not have significant knowledge relating to the allegations against YBM that the Special Committee was investigating. He was able to rely on a due diligence defence.
- Michael Schmidt was YBM's least experienced board member. He was a land surveyor and real estate agent with limited experience raising capital. Although he was on the Special Committee, he assumed a very passive role. The OSC expressed dissatisfaction with this, stating that he could and should have done more on the Special Committee. However, it found that it was reasonable for him to rely on experienced counsel and financial advisors since his level of experience would make it more difficult for him to judge the advice as being right or wrong. Keith Davies was not entitled to the same reliance because he was a more experienced director.

Directors' Due Diligence Defence

Much of the YBM decision deals with principles of disclosure required under the Securities Act (Ontario). However, it also deals in considerable detail with availability of a due diligence defence to the various members of YBM's board of directors and in particular the members of the Special Committee. This required the OSC to review in some detail the duty of care to which directors are subject. The following are some of the highlights from this aspect of the decision. The OSC made the following comments following its discussion of the applicability of the "prudent person" test in determining the reasonableness of the directors' diligence and their belief from the perspective of a prudent person in the circumstances:

- The standard of care for directors and officers is not a professional standard nor is it the negligence standard. Each director and officer owes a duty to take reasonable care in the performance of his or her office and in some circumstances that duty will require a director or officer to take action. That action may in some circumstances call for a resignation.

- Directors are not obliged to give continuous attention to the company's affairs. However, their duties are awakened when information and events that require further investigation become known to them. The standard of care encourages responsibility, not passivity.

- Directors act collectively as a board in the supervision of a company. Directors, however, are not a homogenous group. Their conduct is not to be governed by a single objective standard but rather one that embraces elements of personal knowledge and background, as well as board processes. More may be expected of persons with superior qualifications such as experienced businesspersons. As such, not all directors stand in the same position.

- More may be expected of inside directors than outside directors. A CFO who is on the board may be held to a higher standard than one who is not, particularly if he or she is involved in the public offering.

- When dealing with legal matters, more may be expected of a director who is a lawyer-director who may be in a better position to assess the materiality of certain facts.

- Due to improved access to information, more may sometimes be expected of directors depending on the function they are performing, for example those who sit on board committees, such as a special committee or audit committee. An outside director who takes on committee duties may be treated like an inside director with respect to matters that are covered by the committee's work.

PROPOSED REGULATION OF AUDIT COMMITTEES

On June 27, 2003 the Canadian securities regulators (other than British Columbia) released their proposals for regulating audit committees of public companies. "Multilateral Instrument 52-110" (referred to here as the "Proposed Audit Committee Instrument") will require most public companies to have an audit committee with a written mandate that includes certain prescribed responsibilities. Public companies listed on "major exchanges" (such as the TSX, NYSE and Nasdaq) (referred to here as "Listed Corporations") may only have directors on their audit committees who are "independent" and "financially literate". This requirement does not apply to public companies that are listed on the TSX Ventures Exchange or that are not listed on any stock exchange (referred to as "Ventures Corporations").

Both Listed Corporations and Venture Corporations will be required to make certain disclosures about their audit committees in the corporation's "annual information form" (the "AIF"). Although the AIF is not sent to shareholders, it is easily available on SEDAR.

Definition of "Independence"

A director is "independent" for the purposes of the Proposed Audit Committee Instrument if he or she has no direct or indirect material relationship with the corporation. A director's relationship with the corporation (which may include commercial, charitable, industrial, banking, consulting, legal, accounting or familial relationships) is material if, in the view of the corporation's board of directors, the relationship could reasonably interfere with the exercise of the director's independent judgment. However, the Proposed Audit Committee Instrument automatically excludes directors with certain relationships from serving on the audit committee while the relationship exists and for a period of three years after it ends (referred to as the "cooling-off period"). Existing relationships are grandfathered. The following persons are deemed to have relationships that prevent them from being considered independent:

- officers and employees of the corporation (or its parent or any subsidiary or affiliated entity)
- partners, employees or affiliated entities of:

- the corporation's external auditor (past or present) or
- the corporation's internal auditor (past or present)
- executives of another entity, if any of the corporation's executives sit on the compensation committee of that entity, and
- consultants or advisors to the corporation (or any of its subsidiary entities), or partners or executive officers of the consultant or advisor

The Proposed Audit Committee Instrument also assumes that a person whose immediate family member has any of the relationships described above also has a material relationship with the corporation (and is therefore precluded from sitting on the audit committee). There are certain exemptions from the independence requirements for corporations listed on major exchanges. Among them is an exception for corporations that have a controlling shareholder and have an exemption from the independence requirement for individuals who sit on the board of their parent. Officers and employees of the parent company and persons who are an "affiliated entity" of the corporation are still precluded from sitting on the audit committee. However, if the individual would be considered independent of both the corporation and the affiliated entity (except for the fact that he or she sits on the board of the corporation and the affiliated entity), then that individual is not precluded from sitting on the corporation's audit committee.

Financial Literacy

Every member of the audit committee of a Listed Corporation must be "financially literate". The Proposed Audit Committee Instrument defines "financially literate" to mean:

> the ability to read and understand a set of financial statements that present a breadth and level of complexity of accounting issues that are generally comparable to the breadth and complexity of the issues that can reasonably be expected to be raised by the corporation's financial statements.

Audit Committee Financial Expert

The Proposed Audit Committee Instrument will require each Listed Corporation to disclose whether there is an "audit committee financial expert" on its audit committee. An audit committee financial expert is a person who has:

- an understanding of financial statements and the accounting principles used by the corporation to prepare its financial statements
- the ability to assess the general application of such accounting principles in connection with the accounting for estimates, accruals and reserves
- experience preparing, auditing, analyzing or evaluating financial statements that present a breadth and level of complexity of accounting issues that are generally comparable to the breadth and complexity of issues that can reasonably be expected to be raised by the corporation's financial statements, or experience actively supervising one or more persons engaged in such activities
- an understanding of internal controls and procedures for financial reporting, and
- an understanding of audit committee functions

Audit Committee Responsibilities

The audit committee of every reporting corporation must have a written charter setting out its mandate and responsibilities. The Proposed Audit Committee Instrument requires the audit committee to discharge certain responsibilities, which can be grouped under the following headings:

- Independence of the External Auditor—The Proposed Audit Committee Instrument makes the audit committee responsible for:
  - nominating the external auditor
  - setting the compensation of the external auditor
  - overseeing the work of the external auditor (with the external auditor being required to report directly to the audit committee)
  - pre-approving all non-audit services (subject to certain exceptions) to be provided to the corporation or its subsidiary entities by the external auditor (or the external auditor of such subsidiary entities), although delegation of this function is permitted, with reporting back to the audit committee required, and

- reviewing and approving the corporation's hiring policies regarding employees and former employees of the corporation's external auditors (present and past)
- Financial Statements and Financial Information — The Proposed Audit Committee Instrument requires the audit committee to:
  - review the following before its public disclosure:
    - financial statements
    - MD&A, and
    - earnings press releases
  - satisfy itself that there are adequate procedures in place for the review of the corporation's disclosure of financial information derived from the corporation's financial statements (and periodically assess the adequacy of those procedures)
- Whistle Blowing Procedures — The Proposed Audit Committee Instrument requires the audit committee to establish procedures to deal with:
  - complaints the corporation receives about its accounting, internal accounting controls or auditing matters, and
  - employee concerns about accounting or auditing matters

PROPOSALS FOR CEO/CFO CERTIFICATION

On June 27, 2003 the Canadian securities regulators (other than British Columbia) also released their proposals for certification of a public company's financial statements by the chief executive officer and the chief financial officer. "Multilateral Instrument 52-109" (referred to here as the "Proposed Certification Instrument") will require most public companies to:

- file an "Annual Certificate" signed by the CEO and CFO each year relating to the disclosure in the AIF, annual financial statements and annual MD&A. The certificate will state that, based on the knowledge of each of the CEO and CFO, this material does not contain a misrepresentation and that it fairly presents the issuer's financial condition. It will also include certain statements about the issuer's internal and disclosure controls.
- file an "Interim Certificate" signed by the CEO and CFO each quarter relating to the disclosure in the interim financial statements and interim MD&A. This certificate is identical to the

"Annual Certificate", except that it will not include statements about the effectiveness of the disclosure and internal controls as at the end of the period.

During the one year transition period following the date on which the Instrument comes into force, issuers will be required only to file "bare certificates", which do not include certifications with respect to the issuer's internal and disclosure controls.

Each of the Annual Certificate and the Interim Certificate will include the following six paragraphs:

1. Review of Filings — The CEO and CFO must certify that they have reviewed the documents for which they are providing the certification.

2. No Misrepresentation — The CEO and CFO must certify that, based on their knowledge, there is no misrepresentation in the documents included in the filings.

3. Fair Presentation — The CEO and CFO must certify that, based on their knowledge, the Annual Filings (or Interim Filings) "present fairly" the financial condition of the issuer for the applicable period. Unlike the opinion provided by the external auditor on the annual financial statements, the CEO and CFO may not rely on generally accepted accounting principles ("GAAP"). In the view of the securities regulators, "fair presentation" includes but is not limited to the selection and application of appropriate accounting policies and disclosure of financial information that is informative and reasonably reflects the underlying transactions. The CEO or CFO may feel that it is necessary to make disclosure in addition to what is required under GAAP in order to provide investors with a materially accurate and complete picture of a corporation's financial condition, results of operation and cash flows.

4. Internal and Disclosure Controls — The CEO and CFO must certify that they have responsibility for internal controls and disclosure controls and procedures of the issuer as follows:

- that they have designed, or supervised the design of, internal controls and implemented those controls to provide reasonable assurances that the issuer's financial statements are fairly presented in accordance with GAAP, and

- that they have designed, or supervised the design of, disclosure controls and procedures and implemented those controls and procedures to provide reasonable assurances that material information relating to the issuer (including its consolidated subsidiaries) is made known to them by others within those entities.

In the Annual Certificate (but not in the Interim Certificate) the CEO and CFO must also certify that they have evaluated the effectiveness of the issuer's internal controls and disclosure controls and procedures and presented their conclusions regarding the effectiveness of such controls and procedures in the annual MD&A.

5. Disclosure to Audit Committee and Auditor—The CEO and CFO will be required to certify that they have disclosed to their issuer's audit committee and independent auditors any significant control deficiencies, material weaknesses and acts of fraud that involve management or other employees who have a significant role in the internal controls.

6. Changes in Internal Controls—The CEO and CFO must certify that any significant changes to the internal controls must be disclosed in the issuer's annual and interim MD&A.

PROPOSED REQUIREMENTS FOR OVERSIGHT OF PUBLIC COMPANY AUDITORS

The final proposed regulation released by the CSA on June 27, 2003 relates to the oversight of auditors by the Canadian Public Accountability Board (the "CPAB"). The CPAB was established in 2002 as an independent organization to oversee the design, implementation and enforcement of a system of independent inspection of auditors of Canada's public companies.

Multilateral Instrument 52-108 (referred to here as the "Proposed Auditor Oversight Instrument") will require public companies (except in British Columbia) to engage auditors that participate in the CPAB's oversight program and remain in good standing with the CPAB. In most jurisdictions (i.e. other than Alberta, Manitoba and British Columbia) the Proposed Instrument will also impose requirements on public company auditors to participate in the CPAB's oversight program.